LIBRARY FILE:
Making a Success of the School Library

Edited by
Valerie Coghlan, Patricia Quigley, Rosemary Walton

LIBRARY ASSOCIATION OF IRELAND

First published in 1999 by
Library Association of Ireland
53 Upper Mount Street
Dublin 2
Ireland

Copyright © Library Association of Ireland and
Valerie Coghlan, Patricia Quigley, Rosemary Walton, 1999

Design and Layout: Spiral Graphics

ISBN: 0 94603 736 1

Printed in Ireland by Colour Books Ltd.

Acknowledgments

The editors of and contributors to *Library File* wish to thank the following for their support and assistance:

Alun Bevan, An Chomhairle Leabharlanna; Sydney Blain, Principal of the Church of Ireland College of Education; Ann Byrne, Fingal County Libraries; Monica Cregan, Librarian, Ashton Community School, Cork; Aideen Griffin, Fingal County Libraries, Schools Library Service; Paul Harris, County Librarian, Fingal County Libraries; Siobhán Hayes, Fingal County Libraries; Fr. Gerry Hipwell, O.Carm, Moate Community College, Moate, Co. Westmeath; Norma McDermott, Director, An Chomhairle Leabharlanna;Mary McLaughlin, Children's and Schools' Section, Dublin Corporation Public Libraries; Eamonn Murtagh, Department of Education and Science; Anton Trant and Aidan Clifford, Director and Deputy Director, CDVEC Curriculum Development Unit.

Thanks are due to the principals, librarians and students of the following schools, for allowing their libraries to be photographed:

Primary

Scoil an tÁthar Maitiú,
Glen Avenue, Togher,
Cork.

St Ronan's National School,
Deansrath,
Clondalkin,
Dublin 22.

St Brendan's School,
Blackpool
Cork.

Galway County Library
School Library Service

Post-Primary

Maria Assumpta Secondary School,
Pearse Road,
Ballyphehane,
Cork.

The King's Hospital School,
Palmerstown,
Dublin 20.

St Paul's School,
Walkinstown,
Dublin 12.

Ashton Comprehensive School,
Blackrock Road,
Cork.

Liberties College,
Bull Alley,
Dublin 8.

Moate Community School,
Moate,
Co. Westmeath.

Table of Contents

APPENDICES

Foreword

FOREWORD BY THE MINISTER FOR EDUCATION AND SCIENCE

I am delighted to welcome the publication of *Library File: Making a Success of the School Library* by the Library Association of Ireland. Libraries of all kinds are central to organising and disseminating knowledge and information, but school libraries also have a critical role in cultivating an interest in and a love for reading.

I agree that access to a repository of books and information resources is very important for both teachers and students. At the primary school level, the classroom library is an immediate and convenient source of books and learning materials for children. The use of the classroom library to support the implementation of the curriculum is essential to developing independent learning skills and the classroom library is a central resource in the teaching of reading.

In the larger primary schools where accommodation is provided to organise a central library, children can gain first-hand experience of the way in which books are organised in a library and thus increase their ability to locate information independently. In post primary schools where there are large numbers of students undertaking a wide range of courses, a well-stocked library can enrich and extend the quality of the students' learning by providing a valuable support for collective and collaborative learning.

I welcome the prominence given to school planning in this publication. In the light of the range of information resources available at present, it is vital that all school authorities plan for the use of books and information and communication technologies in the education process. I am confident that the suggestions made in this book will be of considerable practical benefit to school authorities and teachers embarking on updating their school library policies, particularly in the context of the considerable additional resources which have been sent to schools for the purchase of library books. Equally, I am sure that all teachers will find the discussion of the practical issues about selecting and organising books and other library materials very helpful.

Mícheál Martin

Micheál Martin, T.D.,

Minister for Education & Science

Introduction

School libraries are often referred to by terms which imply their central role in the education of young people, terms such as 'engine rooms of education' and 'the foundations of the curriculum'. The intention behind this publication is to present education authorities, school principals, teachers, management bodies and parents with an insight into what constitutes an effective school library. At the same time, it will provide librarians, teachers and all those involved in the setting up and running of a school library with practical guidance on how to do this.

A number of publications are available which provide instruction in the theory and practice of school library organisation and management, but none looks in detail at the role of libraries in the context of the Irish primary and post-primary education system. A previous publication of the Library Association of Ireland, *School libraries: Guidelines for Good Practice* (1994)[1], outlined desirable levels of provision, and another LAI publication, *Library Development in Second Level Schools* (1994)[2], presented a number of practical approaches to aspects of school library organisation. Both of these publications provided valuable information and support, but it is now apparent that what is required is a more comprehensive setting-out of strategies which will lead to the development of high-quality libraries in schools throughout Ireland. The Library Association of Ireland is pleased that with the support of the Department of Education and Science, *Library File: Making a Success of the School Library* will be available in every primary and second-level school. Thus it should be a means of helping to ensure that every young person has equality of access to all the benefits of a good library, regardless of circumstances.

At present access to libraries in schools is unequal. Some schools have well-resourced and managed libraries; others have no libraries at all. The report on reading literacy presented by Michael O. Martin and Mark Morgan[3] clearly indicates that students who have access to a reasonable level of books and other reading materials become better readers than those who do not. The report also shows that providing libraries in the school and in the wider community is the best way of improving reading standards.

A successful library in a school fulfils a number of important functions. These include:

- Serving as a resource bank for the information requirements of the whole school community
- Developing students' skills in information retrieval and management
- Playing an active role in delivering the curriculum
- Encouraging reading for personal, social and cultural development
- Developing students' reading abilities for a variety of purposes.

The Library Association of Ireland in its *Policy Statement on School Library Services*[4] stresses the importance of establishing posts for professional school librarians in all post-primary and large primary schools. In addition all primary schools should have access to the expertise of librarians through the Local Authority School Library Services. While it is not always the reality, it is desirable also that each school has its own separate space for a library, particularly in the case of larger primary schools and all post-primary schools. Whatever the circumstances or conditions pertaining in their schools, it is intended that *Library File* will provide its readers with ideas, information and inspiration for revitalising their libraries.

Each of the contributors to *Library File* is a qualified librarian with considerable experience in different areas of school library development. Their services were contributed on a voluntary basis and considerable thanks is due to them, to Micheál Martin, Minister for Education and Science, to the Executive of the Library Association of Ireland and to all those listed as 'Friends of School Libraries'. Special thanks is due to Liz Turley and Marjory Sliney who have made considerable efforts to ensure that *Library File* is published.

Valerie Coghlan, Patricia Quigley, Rosemary Walton
Editors

[1] School Library Development Ad-hoc Committee. *School Libraries: Guidelines for Good Practice*. Library Association of Ireland, 1994.

[2] Hanrahan, F., ed. *Library Development in Second Level Schools*. Library Association of Ireland, 1994.

[3] Martin, M.O. & Morgan, M. Reading Literacy in Irish Schools.: a comparative analysis. *Irish Journal of Education*, Vol. 28, 1994.

[4] *Policy Statement on School Library Services*. Library Association of Ireland, 1996.

Policy

A policy helps to define what the library is about. It will also help to clarify what its role should not be. This is useful in a situation where, for example, members of staff may see the library as a secretarial or photocopying service.

A library policy should be in sympathy with the policies and broad aims of the school.

It will be derived from the ethos of the school, the requirements of the curriculum, the educational, social and cultural needs of the users.

It will define the library's user groups: teachers, students, management and possibly other groups in the wider community, depending on circumstances.

The policy will form a basis for a Development Plan for the future of the library (see Chapter 2 The School Library Development Plan).

CONSIDERATIONS IN FORMULATING A LIBRARY POLICY

The policy should be drawn up in consultation with others – the principal, teachers, the Board of Management. Creating a policy is an excellent way of promoting discussion about the role and function of the library.

It should:

- be a written document
- be brief
- be circulated widely and made available to every one in the school
- be reviewed regularly and changed where necessary
- reflect the role of the library as the primary source of information provision within the school
- state the library's role in the provision of material for leisure reading.

The policy will provide a rationale for an annual budget and help to define priorities for purchase.

The following considerations will be reflected in the policy:

- Library opening hours
- Financial provision for the library
- What material should be stocked by the library
- The development of the library collection
- The promotion of reading

- ICT in the library
- Library and information skills
- Special needs,
- Organisation of resources
- Evaluation of stock and services
- The composition and role of the library committee

It may be necessary to develop separate policies for some of the above.

Remember, it is important that those involved with the library make known its policy before others who are not involved decide what library policy might be.

SUGGESTIONS FOR FURTHER READING

Dunne, John, *Establishing a Primary School Library Policy*, Swindon: School Library Association, 1994. ISBN 0900641711

Scott, Elspeth, *Establishing a Secondary School Library Policy*, Swindon: School Library Association, 1996. ISBN 0900641754

The School Library Development Plan

THE PLANNING PROCESS

There are two stages in drawing up any plan: the **strategic** and the **operational**. **Strategic Planning** means standing back and looking at where you are now, where you want to get to and what you have to do to get there. **Operational** or **Action Planning** is more concerned with the day-to-day running of the library and is frequently the only sort of planning carried out in school libraries.

Strategic planning is often neglected in school libraries. Providing a service takes precedence over any attempt to stand back and look at where the library is now and where it might be going in the future. Sometimes the culture of the school may not be sympathetic towards planning that is not focused on immediate requirements. Or, it may be difficult to plan for library development because plans for the school's development are uncertain.

Effective planning must involve others in the school and not just the librarian or the teacher with a post of responsibility. Depending on the culture of the school, management, governors, parents, teachers or students may be involved in drawing up the plan. You might consider forming a **Library Committee** or planning group to help with the planning process.

The timespan for a plan may vary, but three years is a reasonable length of time, depending on the scope of the plan. As one plan draws to a close, another should be underway.

RATIONALE FOR PLANNING

A plan provides:
- a focus of attention on aims and objectives
- a means of establishing priorities for funding
- a basis for establishing accountability at all levels
- a rationale for collecting information
- a way of preventing problems from becoming future crises
- an increased awareness of the status of the library
- a means of evaluating your library service.

A plan should:

- be systematic, proactive and participative
- create structures which allow for the setting of aims
- allow for situations which may change
- be flexible when necessary
- be introduced in stages
- prioritise needs: short, medium and long-term
- improve communications within the school and with management bodies and parents
- focus on outcomes
- be written down
- be realistic.

Factors to be considered before drawing up a plan

- How will it fit with any other plan already in operation in the school?
- Time out will be needed to create the plan. This may involve closing the library for a period of time.

Remember, sometimes things get worse before they get better.

MAKING THE PLAN

The most difficult part of planning is getting started. Management guru Tom Peters advises, 'To get going, get going'. In other words, put something down on paper and don't worry about how good it is. It will probably have to be changed later on anyway.

GATHERING INFORMATION

To begin, a situation audit may be carried out in order to reveal current levels of library provision. All aspects of the library's services and activities should be audited. The sections in this publication provide headings under which an audit may be put in place, and they will provide guidelines for the development of your library.

Further information is then required to begin the planning process. This may be obtained by the following:

- Devising and circulating questionnaires in order to establish current levels of satisfaction with the library and likely future requirements
- Gathering statistics related to loans, requests for information, numbers of people using the library
- Establishing what staff/students/management want from the library
- Identifying Strengths, Weaknesses, Opportunities, Threats (SWOT) in relation to the library
- Becoming aware of factors outside and inside the school which will influence the plan, e.g. the introduction of a new curriculum.

Once the plan has been established, it will be necessary to prioritise the present and future needs of the library and its services. For example, if a library is to be computerised, it is best to buy the cataloguing module before a lot of new resources are added to stock. The circulation module may then be added at a later date.

MISSION STATEMENT

Developing a Mission Statement will help to give focus to the plan.

This is a broad philosophical statement of the intent of the library and should be in line with the Mission Statement of the school.

It considers both short-term and long-term needs and highlights the importance of seeing the forest rather than individual trees. For example, is the physical organisation of the resources rather than the transmission of the information contained in the resources the present focus of the library's activities? If so, the Mission Statement will help to bring the focus back to what should be the main purpose of the library.

Having defined the mission of the library, **aims, objectives** and **tasks** can then be developed.

AIMS

Aims should be:
- long-term and capable of conversion into more specific objectives
- divided into categories, e.g. Services; Resources; Technology
- placed in an overall time-frame for completion – short, medium and long-term.

OBJECTIVES

Objectives are the specific interpretation of aims. They:
- require agreement from those who will be involved
- must relate to each other
- should have deadlines for their completion
- should be costed
- should be written down
- should be realistic.

TASKS

Tasks are specific jobs to be carried out to fulfil an objective.

They separate the urgent from the important. It is, however, essential that tasks which are important, even if not required for completion within a specific timescale, are not neglected in favour of jobs which demand immediate attention. This is the difference between thoughtful planning and crisis management.

EVALUATING THE SCHOOL LIBRARY

It is important to evaluate the library service you provide on a regular, preferably annual, basis. A development plan is a useful means of evaluating your library service because it provides:

- a sense of an overall purpose
- a process for gathering information and statistics
- a clear picture of who is responsible for what
- a means of comparison between objectives and their outcomes
- a way of identifying potentially difficult aspects of library organisation.

Remember, when you evaluate, you need to look at both

- **quantifiable** factors: how much? how many? when?

and

- **qualitative** factors: is it effective? does it lead to happier staff/students? does it provide value for money?

The above are inter-related in a well-run library.

AND FINALLY...

- Take time for planning.
- Consult widely, but remember **you** will have to make the decisions.
- Understand that planning may create a fear of change in some individuals.
- Even if school management style is top-down, the production of a plan ensures that management has the necessary information to make decisions.
- Cultivate an advocate for the library on the school board/parents' committee.

ANNUAL REPORT

It is useful to produce an annual report of the library's activities, not only for the purpose of evaluation, but also for the purpose of accountability. An annual report outlines developments in the service, and can be most useful in helping to make a case to the principal and Board of Management for extra funding, additional space or staffing. It is important to stress the positive developments and successful activities which have taken place in the library during the year, before pointing out any problems and asking for extra resources.

You could include the following statistics:

- Number of registered users
- Number of items borrowed
- Number of reference enquiries
- Number of occasions IT equipment was used
- Number of items reserved for users
- Number of class visits
- Number of special events (author visits etc)
- Number of hours open
- Number of new items added to stock.

Computerised library management systems can provide you with this information more quickly and efficiently.

It is important to remember that any report or presentation of statistics must also stress that many library users do not conduct a transaction, and, therefore, are not recorded in the statistics, i.e. the library may be used extensively for consultation and study.

Make a note of activities, events and improvements as they happen over the year; it is very difficult to recall everything at the end of the summer term, when you come to compile the report.

If you organise any events such as an author visit, do remember to take photographs of the occasion, as these enliven an annual report and make it more readable. Even the introduction of new shelving or a new computer should be mentioned and, here again, photographs can convey so much, so quickly to a busy Board of Management. Favourable comments from staff, students or parents should also be quoted in the report. Above all your annual report should look professional and convey an image of the school library as a vibrant centre of learning.

SUGGESTIONS FOR FURTHER READING

Robertson, Stewart, *Development Planning for the School Library Resource Centre*, Swindon: School Library Association, 1993. ISBN 0900641673

Financial Planning in the School Library

Many improvements may be made in a school library by careful planning, attention to efficient routines, making the most of resources by promotional activities and the introduction of an information skills course. However, adequate financial support is an essential ingredient for success. School library funding must ROAR: it must be Realistic, On-going, Agreed and Regular. To obtain this, and to ensure that funds are used in the most effective way, it is necessary to draw up budgets and to make financial plans, both for capital and on-going expenditure.

ESSENTIAL FACTORS IN FINANCIAL PLANNING

Take Time
- Financial planning is too important to be rushed.

Gather Information
- How is the school funded?
- Who are the financially influential people?
- What is the best time of year to look for funds?
- Are there any sources to which you can apply for finance for special projects, e.g. endowment funds, capital grants, sponsorship?
- How will curriculum and other developments affect the need for library resources?
- What are users' requirements?

Communicate Information
- Provide information about the library – promoting the library helps to attract funding.
- Show how well money has been spent in the past (if it has!).
- Demonstrate the need for further funding.

PREPARING A FINANCIAL PLAN

The main areas of expenditure (this assumes that salaries, building maintenance, telephones, etc are paid for by other means) are as follows:

- Capital items – building, furniture, major items of equipment
  These may be once-off capital payments or may be factored in to the
  budget on an incremental basis. Equipment may be leased.
- Administrative expenses – stationery, maintenance contracts
  These are usually on-going expenditure, but may need extra outlay for
  a new or refurbished library.
- Resources – books, software, audio-visual items
  These should be purchased on a planned basis, i.e. allocations should
  be made on an annual basis for different areas of the curriculum and
  for cultural and leisure interests. Specific areas may receive extra
  allocations from year to year. Allow for the replacement of out-dated,
  worn or missing stock.
- Journals and newspapers
  These may be purchased through a newsagent and paid for weekly or
  monthly, or supplied through a subscription agent and paid for on an
  annual basis in advance. The latter option may make it easier to
  budget, but means a commitment for a year.
- Subscriptions to organisations
  These are usually annual.
- Discretionary spending – promotional activities, author visits
  These should be factored in on an annual basis, but the possibility of
  getting special funding for events should be investigated.

Remember to:

- cost proposed items for capital expenditure
- get alternative quotations
- include VAT and postage charges where appropriate
- allow for increases in costs each year
- allow for currency differentials and costs of bank drafts.

Consider using a computer spreadsheet package for the management of
library finances.

RECOMMENDED SPENDING PER STUDENT

The Book Trust (UK) recommends in its 1998 report, *School Spending on
Books*, the following expenditure on books for school libraries:

	Primary Schools	Second-level Schools – Junior Cycle (12–15 yrs)	Second-level Schools – Senior Cycle (16–18yrs)
Adequate provision	£14	£16	£25
Good provision	£16	£19	£30

Establishing the Library

LOCATION

The school library should be a **separate** area, not used for other activities, and not used as a thoroughfare. There are important reasons why the library should be given its own space:

- The library is a learning centre where essential skills, which have application throughout the curriculum, can be developed.
- It means that resources can be centralised and controlled.
- The library must be a quiet area if it is to be used for reading and study.
- It is important that students see the library given the status it deserves.
- For many students, the school library is their first introduction to the world of books and libraries.

The role of the library as a resource for the whole school should be emphasised by locating it centrally within the school, in an area accessible to all students. Signposting within the school will increase the library's visibility and make an important statement about its role. In a multi-storey school, the library should be situated, if possible, on the ground floor; this will facilitate both access by users and the delivery of books and equipment.

The location of the library may well be the single most important factor affecting its usage. It may also be a factor over which you have no control. However, opportunities for re-location may arise as a school develops.

CLASSROOM LIBRARIES

In some schools it is the practice to keep collections, particularly of fiction and basic reference material, in individual classrooms. Such collections should not be seen as substituting for the central library, which should be the main resource area. Classroom libraries are, however, the reality for many smaller primary schools and much of what is suggested in this publication may apply to the development of these collections. The area of the classroom devoted to the library should invite students to browse and use the books available, and the collection should be refreshed on a regular basis.

PHYSICAL AREA

The accommodation requirements of school libraries will vary with the size and circumstances of the school. It is important to be aware of standards and guidelines so that a case may be made for increased space if needed.

There should be space and facilities for studying and for browsing, with sufficient seating space for **10 per cent** of the school population, or **a whole class**, at a time.

The International Federation of Library Associations (IFLA) has made the following recommendations in relation to minimum space requirements for school libraries serving various student populations:

Students	Basic Area *	Total Area *
1–250	1000 sq. ft (93m^2)	1700 sq. ft (159.2m^2)
250–500	2000 sq. ft (186m^2)	4981 sq. ft (463.34m^2)
501+	3000 sq. ft (279m^2)	6181 sq. ft (574.99m^2)

* The basic area refers to the area used for:

- shelving of resources
- reading
- viewing and listening.

* The total area includes, in addition, areas used for other purposes, such as:

- circulation control
- exhibition and display areas
- workroom
- browsing space
- storage
- librarian's office.

The school library should have at least some of the above; the larger the library, the more such areas it is likely to have.

The Library Association of Ireland has recommended that second-level school libraries should occupy a minimum space of 130 sq. metres (1400 sq. ft), and that there should be a minimum of one study seating space per ten students.

Details of the above guidelines are available from An Chomhairle Leabharlanna (see Appendix 3).

APPEARANCE

The physical appearance of the library is very important:

- It must be bright and attractive.
- It should be well-lit, with as much natural light as possible.
- Attractive colours should be used on the walls, furniture and fittings.
- The imaginative use of posters and friezes can enhance the appearance greatly.
- The floor covering should be easy to maintain and should absorb noise.
- Mats and beanbags could be used to create quiet, relaxing areas.

Second-level students will be more focused on examinations and will tend to use their school library more as a study centre than as a leisure area – though the recreational role of the library should still be emphasised. Just as the primary school library gives pupils an introduction to the world of libraries, the second-level school library introduces students to a more 'serious' library, and to the concept of using a library as a research tool. The layout should include study and browsing areas with appropriate seating and tables, a display area and facilities for group work.

SIGNAGE

It is important that you let people know the location of the library and, within the library, the location of each area and section. Plastic or metal signs may be purchased, or signs may be produced on computer and laminated.

FURNITURE AND FITTINGS

A CHECKLIST OF FURNITURE REQUIRED IN A SCHOOL LIBRARY

- Shelves – wall and island units
- Filing cabinet – for project and information files
- Periodical/magazine stand
- Newspaper rack
- Swivel stand – for paperback fiction
- Kinder boxes (for picture books in primary schools)
- Rack for Big Books (in primary schools)
- Chart/map cabinets
- Storage boxes – for artefacts
- CD racks
- Reading desks and/or carrels
- Comfortable chairs and/or beanbags or cushions for relaxed reading
- Issue desk and chair
- Workstations for OPACs and other computers, VCRs and audio-cassette recorders
- Trolley
- Display tables or stands
- Display boards
- Storage cupboards for use of library staff
- Kick steps

SHELVING

A wide variety of shelving material is available, in both wood and metal. Choosing between wood and metal is a matter for individual preference. It is possible to purchase metal shelving with wooden end-panels. No matter what type of shelving you choose it should be **adjustable for height**. A mixture of flat and sloping shelving is recommended, to allow for a versatile display of material. All flat shelving should be provided with shelf-stops, so that books do not fall over, or fall off. Up-and-over sloping shelving (see photograph, p.31) is a useful way of displaying and storing magazines.

Wall shelving should be safely and securely mounted, and free-standing (or island) shelving should be safe and properly balanced.

Recommended Heights of Shelving in School Libraries (Library Association, UK)	
Lower Primary School	120 cm
Upper Primary School	150 cm
Second-Level School	195 cm

- The recommended shelf length is **90cm**.
- Standard depths are **20cm, 22cm, 25cm** and **30cm** – the latter are necessary for the shelving of large books.

To determine the quantity of shelving required for the library's stock, the following estimates of capacity per standard 90cm shelf may be of assistance:

- General fiction and non-fiction: 30-36 books
- Reference material: 18 books
- Picture books: 36-42 books
- Face-out display: 3-4 books.

Calculations should be based on shelves being no more than 80 per cent full. If shelves are too tightly-filled, books may be damaged, it will be difficult to shelve or extract books, and there will be no room for new material.

SEATING

Tables and chairs of appropriate heights for students of all ages in the school should be provided. The following is an indication of suitable heights for seating and tables for students of various ages:

Age	Seat Height	Table Height
5–7	320mm (12.5 in.)	550mm (21.5 in.)
7–9	360mm (14 in.)	600mm (23.5 in.)
9–13	390mm (15 in.)	650mm (25.5 in.)
13–Adult	445mm (17 in.)	700mm (27.5 in.)

Comfortable low chairs, cushions or beanbags may be made available.

RESOURCES

Where to Start

Very often, the teacher or librarian who is asked to set up a school library is faced with a room full of books which are in disarray, so the challenge is to put order on chaos. The following steps are recommended:

Step One: Centralise

Collect books and non-book material from all the classrooms and staff rooms in the school and centralise everything. In a primary school it is desirable to have classroom libraries as adjuncts to the main library. Books in the classroom library should be recorded in the library catalogue and their location indicated. These collections should be refreshed from the main library stock on a regular basis.

Step Two: Categorise

Find out what types of material you have in stock.
The following categories should apply:

- Fiction
- Non-fiction (information) books
- Packs
- Ring-binders
- Reference books (encyclopedias, dictionaries, atlases, etc.)
- Maps
- Charts
- Slides and photographs
- Audio-cassettes
- Videos
- Magazines
- CD-ROMs
- Periodicals
- Newspapers
- Artefacts.

Step Three: Evaluate

While sorting the material, you should also assess its age and condition.

- Weed out dated materials.
- If the books are in poor condition, throw them out.

The sorting and weeding (stock editing) you do at this stage will provide a solid foundation on which to develop your library.

Recommendations on the size of a school's library stock vary widely and will obviously depend largely on funding. Recommendations range from 20 items per student to a more realistic figure of 5 items per student. The library should have enough books to ensure that:

- each student can have at least one item on loan
- some material is still available for reference
- some material is available for class/group work.

It is desirable that, initially, the library should have no fewer than two books per student. This should be increased as soon as funding allows and requirements are established.

The following tables offer an indication of the minimum stock levels recommended by the Library Association (UK).

FOR SCHOOLS OF 240 STUDENTS OR LESS:	
AGE GROUP	MINIMUM NUMBER OF UNITS OF STOCK
5–11	2640
11–16	3120
16+	4560

FOR SCHOOLS OF MORE THAN 240 STUDENTS						
AGE GROUP	UNITS PER STUDENT	PUPILS: 500 750 1000 1500 EXAMPLE OF NUMBER OF UNITS OF STOCK RECOMMENDED				
5–11	11	5500	8250	11000	
11–16	13	6500	9750	13000	19500
16+	19	9500	14250		

Remember: the figures recommended above are the absolute minimum.

STORAGE AND DISPLAY

Ensure that the library looks well – it should be attractive and welcoming, and a good display of books and non-book material is the key to providing that atmosphere.

It is important that the shelves are kept tidy and well-ordered so that students can easily find what they want.

Books

- Fiction should be shelved in alphabetical sequence by author surname.
- Non-fiction books should be shelved by subject.

Non-book material

There should be storage and display facilities not only for books (including picture books and Big Books in primary schools) but also for magazines and all the other media which make up the stock of a library. These are likely to include audio-cassettes, video-cassettes, CDs, CD-ROMs, posters, slides, maps, project packs, games, information files.

Pamphlet boxes are very useful for the storage of leaflets, pamphlets, maps, etc.

Filing Cabinets

A filing cabinet (or cabinets) will be an essential storage facility in a school library. This will contain project files, photographs, press cuttings, looseleaf information and other ephemeral material which is most conveniently stored in folders, either cardboard or transparent plastic, and hung in a filing cabinet. Material in packs and folders should be classified by subject and arranged chronologically within the subject. Both the packs and the hanging files should be clearly labelled and the contents of packs should be listed on the outside of the folder. Slide packs may also be hung in filing cabinets.

Magazine/Periodical Racks

Magazine swivel stands or lift-up (up-and-over) shelves (see photograph) should be used for displaying magazines and journals. Current issues should be displayed and back issues should be kept in pamphlet boxes or under the lift-up shelves.

Storage Boxes

Artefacts such as equipment or models used in the teaching of history, geography, and science, may be kept in the library. If so, they should be contained in individual plastic wallets of appropriate size with zip tops. These should be labelled with the title of the contents and bar-coded if a computer system is in operation.

Chart Racks or Cabinets

Large racks for hanging charts and maps are available from library suppliers.

Kinder Boxes

Kinder boxes, which are deep storage boxes divided into compartments, typically 60cm (2 ft) square, are particularly suitable for holding large illustrated books.

Swivel Stands

Swivel stands, which permit the display of material on rotating stands, are particularly suitable for paperbacks. They can also be used to house non-book materials such as audio and video cassettes, talking books and CD-ROMs. In the case of such non-book materials, only the empty boxes should be displayed and the contents kept at the issue desk. Swivel stands should be secure and steady.

Display Boards

Display boards, to display students' work, the covers of new books, or a particular exhibition, are expensive but are worth it, because they greatly enhance the appearance of the library.

Issue Desk

The general layout of the library should allow maximum supervision from the issue desk.

This should be large enough to accommodate the computer and keyboard (if a computerised issue system is in operation) and to allow space for transactions to take place. It should also have drawers. It is preferable to have a separate office/workroom.

Reputable library furniture suppliers (see Appendix 4) can advise you on the wide range of specialised furniture available and may also provide a library design service.

ACCESS

In order to provide the maximum access you should aim to have the library open for as many hours as possible. However, it is important to remember that many of the tasks of running a school library cannot be carried out while it is being used by students and teachers; time and staff must be allocated accordingly.

ORGANISING VOLUNTARY HELP

You may be able to enlist the help of student and parents in running the library. This involves planning. You must consider carefully the type of work which students could learn to do in the library, and how much training would be involved. Most students and parents enjoy library work and will happily help out with routine tasks, such as covering books, sticking on date labels, issuing and returning books. It would be useful to provide a manual of library procedures and routines for the use of helpers.

REGULATIONS

Establish clear rules for library use – for example, rules regarding eating, drinking and noise levels.

HEALTH AND SAFETY

There should be adequate power points for equipment and these power points should be safely located so that they are not hazardous to young children. Care should be taken to ensure that there are no dangerous trailing cables.

Other matters to consider are the supervision of students in the library when the librarian is not on duty, and what is covered by insurance.

HOMEWORK CLUBS

Many schools and community centres are now running after-school homework clubs. These provide an environment which is supportive to study and sympathetic personnel on hand to give advice and help.

In schools where there is a designated library area this may be a means of extending the role of the library and of increasing the use of the resources. An important factor to be considered is that of supervision. It may not be possible for staff in charge of the library to provide this, and even if it is they will need extra help. In some instance students from local third-level institutions, in particular from Colleges of Education or university Education departments, may be able to assist.

A library based homework club can provide:

- Comfortable surroundings conducive to study
- Access to the library's resources
- Guidance and encouragement for students.

SUGGESTIONS FOR FURTHER READING

Charlton, Leonore, *Designing and Planning a Secondary School Library Resource Centre*, Swindon: School Library Association, 1992.
ISBN 0900641630

Cottrell, Jenny, *Establishing a Homework Club in the Secondary School Library.* Swindon: School Library Association, 1998. ISBN 0900641886

Dewe, Michael, *Planning and Designing Libraries for Young People*, London: Library Association Publishing, 1995. ISBN 185604100X

Library and Information Services Council (Northern Ireland), *Libraries in Post-Primary Schools: Guidelines for Good Practice*, Ballymena: Library and Information Services Council, 1995. ISBN 1872729053

Library and Information Services Council (Northern Ireland), *Libraries in Primary Schools: Guidelines for Good Practice*, 1995. ISBN 1872729045

Managing Resources in the School Library

The efficient and effective management of libraries depends on the setting up and maintenance of systems – ordering, receipting, accessioning, cataloguing, classifying and circulating. These are all discussed in this chapter. While they may all be operated manually, it is strongly recommended that you automate them using a library management system.

LIBRARY ROUTINES – DAY-TO-DAY RUNNING OF THE LIBRARY

ORDERING

Records should be kept of all orders placed. This can be done in a record book, but it is better to use a separate order form for each item (see example below) or to do it by computer. If using forms, they can be filed and then used as a record of accession, when the item is received. The most useful type of order form is an NCR duplicate form. If you use such a form one copy should be sent to the supplier and the other copy filed in your order file or register.

LIBRARY			
For Library use only	Author (Surname First)		
Ordered from	Title		
Date	Publisher	Edition	Year
	Price ISBN		No. of Copies
Received	Requested by		Date
Classification No.	Source		

RECEIPTING

When new items arrive from the supplier, refer to the order form file or register. Check that the item is the one you ordered, and is in good condition.

ACCESSIONING

Every new item should be given an accession number. The accession number is the unique identifying number for each item added to stock. It also distinguishes one copy of the same title from another. The accession number is not the same as the ISBN (International Standard Book Number). The publisher allocates the ISBN. You create the accession number. Not every item has an ISBN but every item (including videos, maps etc) in your library must be given an accession number. A decision regarding the make-up of accession numbers has to be made. It is usually a simple running number. When starting from scratch, the first item to be accessioned can be allocated the number 1 or 0001 etc. The initials of the school could be added, e.g. BS 0001 (BS = Burrow School). Many computerised library systems allocate accession numbers. It is best to use barcodes and a barcode scanner with computerised systems.

An Accessions Register

This is desirable if your system is not computerised. Each new item is listed in the register with its author, title, publisher, supplier, order number, date added to stock, price and, of course, its accession number. All this information should be written on one line of the register. For example:

Accession Number	Author	Title	Publisher	Supplier	Order No.	Date Added	Price
BS 0001	Martell	Na Ceiltigh	An Gúm	Books Inc.	1181	6/4/98	£7.50
BS 0002	Taylor	A Children's Book of Irish Rhymes	Gill & Macmillan	All Books	1182	10/5/98	£6.99
BS 0003	Carroll	Rosie's Gift	Poolbeg	All Books	1182	10/5/98	£3.99

PROCESSING NEW ITEMS

When preparing new items for addition to the library shelves, display stands and cabinets, the following procedures should be carried out:

1. Stamp new stock with school stamp.

2. Attach date label to all loan items.

3. Write accession number near the Dewey Classification number (if applicable) on the reverse of the title page and on the date label.

4. Put Dewey Classification number on the spine of the book.

5. Cover books to prolong their shelf life – ready-made transparent book covers are available from library suppliers.

CATALOGUING AND CLASSIFICATION

The person in charge of the library must know what the stock consists of and must be able to retrieve information from the stock with speed and ease. For these reasons, every library must have a catalogue of all material. The catalogue is the key to accessing information about a library's stock. The catalogue may be either manual (card) or computerised; the latter is more efficient.

MANUAL OR NON-COMPUTERISED CATALOGUE

A catalogue contains bibliographical information about all items regardless of physical format. A catalogue consists of:

- the Author Index
- the Classified Index
- the Subject Index.

The **Author Index** is arranged alphabetically according to author's surname. The **Classified Index** is a listing of all non-fiction items according to their subject matter. Subjects are represented by **classification numbers**, so the cards are filed numerically by classification number. The classification system that is most widely used by public, college and school libraries is the Dewey Decimal Classification system. A library user searching the Classified Index for information on a specific subject will need to know the classification number for the subject. It is necessary, therefore, to have a **Subject Index** to the Dewey Classification system. This index consists of the names of subjects and their corresponding Dewey classification numbers; cards in this index are filed alphabetically.

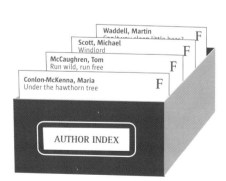

Alphabetical Author Index

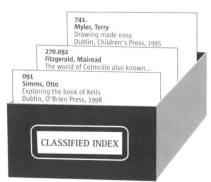

Classified Index

COMPUTERISED CATALOGUE

A computerised catalogue combines all three indexes and so allows many more ways of searching, for example by **title, publisher, series, format, ISBN** or **keyword**. It is therefore a more effective and efficient system by which to retrieve information. A good computerised cataloguing system will allow both global searching (all parts of a record) and searching by field (specified parts of a record).

CATALOGUING

Cataloguing involves creating records for all items in stock regardless of format, i.e. all books and non-book material such as CD-ROMS, video-cassettes, and audio-cassettes.

Each catalogue record comprises bibliographic information such as author, title and publisher. This information should be transcribed exactly as it appears on the title page and the reverse of the title page. Be careful to ensure that the information you give is accurate and that it refers to the particular edition in hand. The **details of description** should be given in the following order:

■ First or main author/editor (personal or corporate)
■ Title, including sub-title
■ Edition
■ Publisher and date of publication
■ Physical description (if a book, whether hardback or paperback; if a non-book, whether audio-cassette, CD-ROM, etc)
■ Series
■ Notes (e.g. 'a documentary', or 'originally published in 19--',)
■ International Standard Book Number.

All this information, as well as the price, the accession number and Dewey Classification number must be included whether you are creating a computerised or a manual catalogue record. In a computerised system each of the above pieces of bibliographic information forms a separate **field** in the catalogue record. In most systems the number and position of fields on the screen are pre-determined.

A basic rule in cataloguing is to consult the **title page** for the full title of the work and name of the author or editor.

Information about the publisher, date of publication, edition, and ISBN must all be taken from the **reverse of the title page.**

CREATING A MANUAL CATALOGUE

Use standard 5"x 3" index cards on which to type the bibliographic details. Type the author's name at the top of the card, putting the author's surname first, followed by the first name. If the item is non-fiction, you will need to type two catalogue cards, one for the Author Index, and the other for the Classified Index; these two cards will be identical. In the case of fiction items, one card will normally suffice.

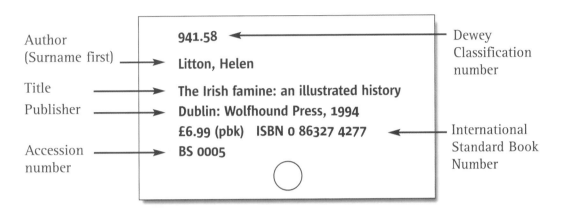

Author (Surname first) →

Title →

Publisher →

Accession number →

941.58 ← Dewey Classification number

Litton, Helen

The Irish famine: an illustrated history

Dublin: Wolfhound Press, 1994

£6.99 (pbk)   ISBN 0 86327 4277 ← International Standard Book Number

BS 0005

Sample Catalogue Card

For the sake of clarity, there should be separate Author Index drawers for fiction and non-fiction.

CLASSIFICATION

A library contains material on a wide range of subjects. It is your responsibility to ensure that library users retrieve information on specific subjects with accuracy and ease. The most efficient way to achieve this is to organise resources according to their content or subject matter, i.e. to shelve items on similar or related subjects in close proximity to each other. The Dewey Decimal Classification (DDC) system enables you to classify stock in this way. It is recommended that you use this system as it is the one most widely used by libraries everywhere. The abridged edition of DDC will be sufficient for the needs of school libraries. The DDC system divides the whole field of knowledge into 9 major classes, plus a class for 'Generalities'. The classes are allocated three-digit numbers ranging from 000–999.

The ten broad subject areas are:

000	Generalities, General Knowledge
100	Philosophy, Psychology
200	Religion
300	The Social Sciences
400	Language, Linguistics
500	Pure Sciences
600	Technology (Applied Sciences)
700	The Arts
800	Literature
900	Geography, History, Biography.

These main classes are then further divided into subclasses. For example '500 Pure Sciences' is divided into the following subclasses:

510	Mathematics
520	Astronomy
530	Physics
540	Chemistry
550	Earth Sciences
560	Palaeontology
570	Life Sciences
580	Botany
590	Zoological Sciences.

It is recommended that you buy the abridged version of the Dewey Decimal Classification system mentioned earlier; in the introduction it explains how to use the system, and in particular how to build classification numbers.

Steps in Classifying

The first task in classifying is to ascertain the subject matter or content of the work in hand.

Get as much information as you can from the item by consulting:

- title and sub-title
- the contents page
- the blurb
- the introduction/preface.

When you are sure of the subject, consult the **Relative Index** to the **DDC** system, the **DDC schedules** and your own **Subject Index**. Choosing the appropriate classification number is important. Remember that items wrongly classified may be 'lost' in the collection.

The chosen classification number is then put on:

- the top of the catalogue cards
- the date label inside the item
- the reverse of the title page
- the spine of the book/item.

In the case of Reference material, include the abbreviation REF in front of the classification number,

e.g. REF023 (English dictionaries).

Because items vary in size and physical format, it is not possible to adhere to a strict shelf arrangement of all non-fiction items by classification number. The Classified Index, however, will bring all these items together. Consulting the Classified Index, rather than going directly to the shelves at the relevant classification number, is the most efficient way of finding out what the library has in stock on specific subjects. Moreover, items may not be on the shelves for a variety of reasons, e.g. they may be on loan or they may be in need of repair.

Subject Index

You must set up and maintain a Subject Index to the DDC system. This Index will consist of classification numbers that have been used in the classification of your library's stock. The Subject Index ensures consistency of cataloguing and it enables users searching for material to consult the Classified Catalogue or to go directly to the shelves at the appropriate shelf number.

Remember, when you are using a classification number for the first time, to type a Subject Index card for it.

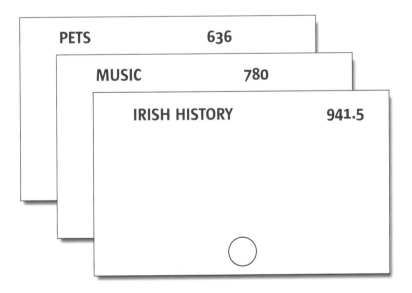

Sample Subject Index Cards

Fiction

It is not necessary to classify fiction. When shelving fiction, books should be arranged alphabetically by author's surname.

TO SUMMARISE

The catalogue:
- is a record of the entire school library's stock
- is a reference tool.

Consulting it enables the user to discover:

- whether the library has a specific title by a particular author
- which items the library stocks by a particular author
- what items the library has on specific subjects
- where items are located.

CIRCULATION SYSTEMS

A circulation system is necessary because you need to have the following information about your stock:

- Who has an item out of the library
- How long it has been out and when it is due back
- Which resources are most in demand and may need to be stocked in multiples
- Students' reading patterns
- Statistical information on what resources are used in the library.

Effective procedures for the loan and return of materials enable schools to keep an accurate account of stock.

A computerised system makes it very easy to check the status of an item, i.e. whether it is out on loan, on order or on reserve. When choosing a computerised system you should ask the following questions:

- Are different loan periods available and can they be easily changed?
- Does it print recall notices?
- Does the system warn of reservations and outstanding loans during a transaction?
- Are records updated immediately following a transaction?

NON-COMPUTERISED CIRCULATION SYSTEMS

The two most practical non-computerised circulation systems are:

1. The User Card system

2. The Book Card (Browne) system.

1. THE USER CARD SYSTEM

How it works

- All users have cards containing details of name and class.
- Each time a book is borrowed the details of the book and the date borrowed are written on the user card (see diagram below).
- The card is than filed in alphabetical order by user name.
- There could be a separate box or tray for each class, or one alphabetical sequence for the whole school.
- When the book is returned, the card is taken out of the file, and a line put through the record of the loan.
- The card can then be filed until the student borrows another book.
- The only equipment needed for this system is a set of 6" x 4" cards, one for each user, and some filing boxes.

Murphy, John		Fifth Class	
Accession/Book Number	Author	Title	Date Borrowed
~~100~~	~~Litton~~	~~The Civil War~~	~~15.4.98~~
~~150~~	~~Barber~~	~~Catkin~~	~~20.6.98~~
200	Deary	Vicious Vikings	21.6.98

Sample User Card

Advantages

- In a small school this is the easiest method.
- The simplicity of the system enables senior students to issue books.
- A clear reading record is kept for each student.
- It is easy to check which items are due for return or are overdue.

Disadvantages

Cards are not filed by title so that searching for an item can be time-consuming.

2. THE BOOK CARD SYSTEM

The User Card system is suitable for small school libraries but can be slow to operate in larger, busier libraries. The Book Card (Browne) system is a more efficient way of recording a large number of loans. This system is widely used in those public libraries which have not been computerised.

How it works

- Each student has a ticket with his/her name and class on it.
- Each book has a date label with a pocket and book card.
- The information written on the book card is as follows :
    - Accession number at the top
    - Classification number (or F if the item is fiction)
    - Author and Title

(see Diagram 1).

- The information written on the date label is as follows :
    - Name of school
    - Classification number/fiction
    - Accession number

(see Diagram 2).

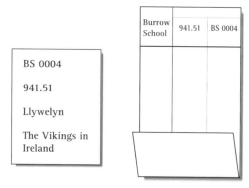

Diagram 1   *Diagram 2*

- Students have to have one ticket for each book borrowed, into which the book cards from the borrowed books are placed.

When a book is borrowed:

- The book card is removed from the date label pocket and placed into the student's ticket (see diagram 3).
- The return date is stamped on the date label.
- The ticket is then filed in the issue tray, in return date order. Within the date, tickets are filed in accession number order (see diagram 4).

When the book is returned:

- The date on the date label is checked and that date in the issue tray is searched.
- The ticket is located by matching the accession number on the date label to the accession number on the book card.

- The ticket is removed from the issue tray.
- The book card is taken out of the student's ticket and placed in the date label pocket of the returned book.
- The ticket is returned to the student.

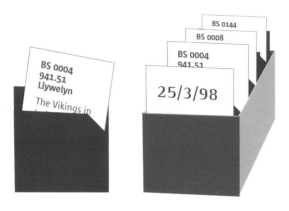

Diagram 3   *Diagram 4*

Advantages

- Books can easily be traced to satisfy specific student requests.
- It is easy to identify overdue books.
- The simplicity of the system enables students to assist in the running of the library.
- Local Authority school library services may already process books for issuing according to the Book Card system.

Disadvantages

- Book cards may easily be lost from the date label pockets.

SUGGESTIONS FOR FURTHER READING

Abridged Dewey Decimal Classification and Relative Index, Edition 12.
Ohio: Forest Press, 1990. ISBN 0910608423

Lemaire, Kathy, *Issue Systems for the Primary School Library,*
Swindon: School Library Association, 1998.
ISBN 0900641894

Libraries in Primary Schools: Guidelines for Good Practice, Ballymena:
Library and Information Services Council (Northern Ireland), 1995.
ISBN 1872729045

Ray, Colin, *Running a School Library.* London: Macmillan, 1994. ISBN
0333526503

Winkel, Lois, (ed.), *Subject Headings for Children; a List of Subject
Headings used by the Library of Congress with Dewey Numbers Added*
(Vol. 1 & 2), New York: First Press, 1994. ISBN 0910608466 (Vol. 1)
ISBN 0910608466 (Vol. 2)

At the time of writing a version of the Dewey Decimal Classification
System for primary schools is in preparation by the SLA. A version for
post-primary schools will follow.

Information and Communication Technology

Information and Communication Technology (ICT) plays a major part in providing access to information in a school library and in disseminating information from the library. It is not the intention of this publication to provide an indepth analysis of how ICT works. Such information goes out of date quickly and there are many excellent publications on the market which give information about the uses of ICT, from beginner to advanced levels. A selection of such publications should be held in the library, but remember that many of them will date rapidly so the stock must be frequently updated.

To enable fast and efficient access to electronically delivered information the library must have computers of a high specification.

One of the most effective uses of ICT in a school library is the automation of library routines and cataloguing procedures. ICT also allows staff and students to search for information using the many options offered by a computerised library system.

COMPUTERISING THE LIBRARY

By introducing an efficient automated library management system (LMS) you will improve the effectiveness of your library. Computerised library systems can automate the routine operations of ordering, cataloguing and circulating materials as well as improving the retrieval of items from stock. However, the decision whether or not to computerise the library should be based on careful analysis of the issues involved. You should consider what services you want the library to provide and what you can reasonably expect from a computerised system, taking into account the benefits, costs and workload involved.

Advantages

Overall, a computerised system enhances the image of the library and increases library use by making users more aware of the resources available. In addition:

- It speeds up routine library tasks.
- The location of all items, particularly those items on loan, is more easily determined.
- Students enjoy searching a computerised catalogue and it allows more ways of searching.
- Specialised reading lists are more easily produced.
- Reservation of resources is simplified.
- It gives practice in modern information retrieval methods.
- It provides a practical example of the use of computers.
- It simplifies the production of overdue (recall) notices.
- It allows for the production of statistics on library use.

Disadvantages

- Cost – computerised library systems are expensive in terms of hardware and software.
- Workload – automating the library is onerous and time-consuming.
- Things get worse before they get better – you may have to close the library for a period in order to computerise.

LIBRARY MANAGEMENT SYSTEMS

There is a range of software available, ranging from general databases designed for business applications, to library management systems designed for libraries. A general database package allows you to create your own databases. However, these require a lot of expertise to set up; they have to be adapted to the needs of the library and are often unable to offer basic library functions such as circulation. Library management systems comprise a number of functional units that correspond to library activities. They generally include the following:

- Acquisition – ordering and receipting stock
- Cataloguing – input of stock details (Remember: you have to input these details!)
- OPAC (Online Public Access Catalogue) – searchable by author, title, subject/keyword etc

- Circulation – issue, return, renewal, reservation and recall
- Registration of journals
- Generation of statistics (report generation).

It is strongly recommended that you install a library management system.

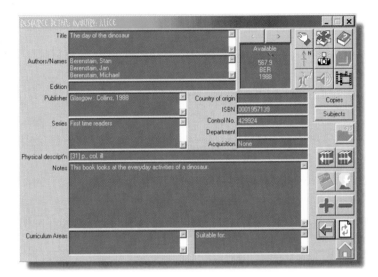

Technical considerations

Most systems operate on PCs. You are advised to buy as powerful a computer as possible because library management systems take up large amounts of space and memory. If you accept the '486 that the IT Department is discarding' you cannot expect your LMS to work at its most effective.

Even if you do not intend to **network** the system in the short term it is worth considering a system that can easily be networked in the future. If you choose to operate your system on more than one computer you will need to buy a multi-user licence. This would enable you to operate, for example, an OPAC on one machine and have another machine at the library desk dedicated to routine library functions.

Most systems now offer a graphical user interface and are menu driven.

Different systems use different methods of backing up data each day. Data must be backed up in case of computer failure.

PLANNING FOR COMPUTERISATION

The selection and installation of a library system is a large undertaking and one that requires the support of the school community. It can be a daunting task and requires considerable analysis and planning.

It is important to brief all stakeholders on the benefits, costs, time scale and procedures. The initial step in the selection procedure is to consider carefully what you require from your system and, following this, to draw up a detailed specification of requirements. Read as much as you can on the topic, visit other libraries and attend any library equipment exhibitions. Use the information gained to identify possible system suppliers and to expand your specification.

Specification

The specification should include such factors as:

- Number of items in stock, present and projected
- Student and teacher numbers, present and projected
- Circulation procedure
- A detailed list of additional functional requirements, e.g. journal control.

The choice you are making is one you will have to live with for a considerable time so do not limit yourself by current requirements, usage and budgets. Outline your ideal system and include all your requirements. Remember, library automation is usually followed by an increase in usage.

Selection Process

Contact system suppliers (see Appendix 4) for details of their systems and request a demonstration disk, a list of local libraries in which the product is being used, and detailed product descriptions. Compare this information with your specification to produce a shortlist of systems. At this stage it is worthwhile visiting other libraries and talking to the library staff there to get an insight into how the system performs. It may be useful to include influential stakeholders – principal, member of Board of Management, ICT specialist in your school – in these visits. You must consider the following important questions:

General

- How easy is it to use?
- Is there good support available from the supplier?
- What training is supplied?
- Are screens attractive and well laid out?
- Is the next step in a procedure prompted?
- How is data backed up on a daily basis? (vital, in case the computer crashes)
- Is supporting documentation comprehensive and easily understood?
- Are system upgrades available? – and are they expensive?
- Do other users recommend the product?
- Is there a user group?

OPAC (Online Public Access Catalogue)

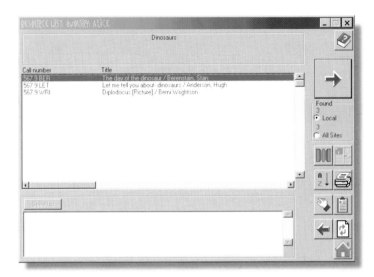

- Can it be easily used by all age groups, with simple screens and help available?
- Can it be demonstrated to new users quickly and easily?
- Can it search all parts of a record (global search) as well as specified sections (field), i.e. title, author, class number, subject or keyword?
- How quick is response time?
- Is a message or icon used to indicate that a search is in progress?
- Is an advanced search option available?

Library Routines

- Are different loan periods available and can they be easily changed?
- Does it print recall notices?
- Does the system warn of reservations and outstanding loans during a transaction?
- Are records updated immediately following a transaction?
- Is it possible to print out records?
- Is input by barcode scanner and by keyboard possible?
- Are statistics produced on usage by class number and user groups?
- Is there fast input of details for circulation?
- Are records easily edited?
- In what format are daily back-up records produced?

Selection

Following the review of documentation and library visits, draw up an assessment report for each product and use this, together with your specification, to negotiate with suppliers and to make that final decision. You will not find everything you want in any one system. All the options available in each system must be balanced against the quality and availability of supplier support and against your budget.

Hardware

Regardless of the size of a school and of the ICT equipment in the school, the minimum amount of equipment in the school library should be:

- A PC dedicated to library operations
- A colour printer
- A telephone line/ISDN and a modem to access the Internet and other resources
- At least one PC with CD-ROM drive
- A scanner.

INFORMATION SKILLS

Often when introducing electronic systems to the school library there is a danger of over-emphasising technology at the expense of training and skill enhancement. It is essential to ensure that teachers and students participate in an appropriate information skills programme. The basic computer skills and techniques should be provided in the context of enhancing students' ability to select, evaluate and use information (see Chapter 8 on Information Skills in the School Library). Students and staff using CD-ROMs or the Internet should understand search techniques and the steps involved in conducting an information search. Efficient use will be encouraged if 'help' sheets instructing users how to carry out information searches are left beside each computer.

It may also be necessary to have a policy which states that only those who are experienced in basic search methodologies may use the equipment. Otherwise, the library may assume a training role in IT handling and this may be difficult to sustain.

CD-ROM

When considering CD-ROMs for the school library, thought should be given to the information provision role of the library. There are many excellent educational products which are teaching aids but these may belong in the computer room or classroom or in subject departments in post-primary schools. Increasingly, encyclopedias and reference material are available on CD-ROM. These are usually cheaper than hard copies and can be updated more often. Therefore, consideration should be given to purchasing CD-ROM versions of encyclopedias and some specific reference material. Reviews of CD-ROMs are found in a number of the reviewing journals. The quarterly journal *The School Librarian* devotes a number of pages to reviews of CD-ROMs and Internet sites. A local area network within the library may enable a number of students to use a CD-ROM at the same time.

INTERNET

The Internet can be used to access information in a variety of ways:

- Webpages on a huge number of subjects
- Remote access to the catalogues of other libraries
- Current awareness services
- Commercial databases
- Mailing lists, newsgroups and discussion lists.

Students should be reminded that information found on the Internet may not always be reliable.

Introducing the Internet

The introduction of the Internet should be carefully planned as there are a number of matters which will need careful consideration:

- Cost: searching can be expensive, especially during the daytime.
- A dedicated ISDN telephone line will be required if there is not already one in the school.
- Who will provide users with training in searching techniques?
- Who will maintain the equipment?
- Will students be allowed e-mail access in the library?

Access to the Internet

It may be necessary to develop a policy with regard to who has access to computers in the library, and in particular with regard to Internet access. Questions which will have to be answered include the following:

- Do all staff and students have unregulated access?
- Is access available only to staff and to students above a certain level?
- Will time spent searching the Internet be regulated?

By using a booking form, time spent on a library computer may be reserved in advance and may also be limited. This would allow for the specific allocation of time and would ask users to indicate broadly what they are searching for.

Some studies have found that in co-educational schools girls tend to be dominated by boys when seeking access to computers. It is important to ensure that all groups in the school have appropriate access and do not feel intimidated in any way when using computers.

It may be necessary to install software which will filter undesirable sites. There are a number of packages available, but they are not always totally successful.

A data bank of useful URLs (Uniform Resource Location) may be built up by asking students to 'bookmark' sites which have yielded information of value. This might in due course be printed out for circulation or left beside the computers. Short annotations indicating the interest level and likely use of a site would be a helpful addition.

Staff and students should be encouraged to save Internet searches onto floppy disks, to be downloaded at a later stage.

ELECTRONIC BIBLIOGRAPHICAL INFORMATION

A number of library management systems provide a facility which enables students to check for books which they might enjoy reading by using a detailed search system related to genre, age of student, reading age of the text, etc.

It is also possible to purchase bibliographic information on CD-ROM, e.g. *Times Educational Supplement BookFind*. This may be linked to the library management system to help with cataloguing.

ADMINISTRATIVE USES OF COMPUTERS IN THE SCHOOL LIBRARY

It will be useful to use computers in the library for routine and administrative purposes. Word processing, desktop publishing and spreadsheet software can enhance the production and presentation of reports, training materials and publicity.

A computer linked to a multimedia projector will be an asset when providing training in library and information skills.

ONGOING FUNDING

Library staff will require training on a regular basis in order to keep up with developments in ICT. The ICT itself will need to be upgraded regularly to keep pace with technological developments. Therefore, ongoing funding is required for the maintenance and upgrading of both skills and hardware.

SUGGESTIONS FOR FURTHER READING

Dubber, Geoff, (ed.), *The Internet, the Secondary School Library and the Independent Learner,* Swindon: School Library Association, 1999.
ISBN 0900641878

Scott, Elspeth, *Managing the Internet in the School Library*, Swindon: School Library Association, 1997. ISBN 0900641819

Selecting Resources for the School Library

The school library collection should complement the curriculum and reflect the leisure interests of students and staff. Collection development is the process of expanding and improving the resources of a library.

There are a number of definable elements to the collection development process and these can be listed as follows:

- Assessment of present and future requirements
- Policy
- Selection
- Acquisition
- Stock editing
- Evaluation.

ASSESSMENT OF PRESENT AND FUTURE REQUIREMENTS

To develop a library's collection, it is essential to define the needs of the users of that library. It is important to determine:

- the educational and recreational information needs of students
- the educational and management information needs of teachers
- the age profile of students
- the accessibility of public library services and other information services (including electronic) to students and teachers after school hours
- the resources which may already be available within the school
- curricular developments.

POLICY

A written collection development policy should be the norm for school libraries as it can greatly assist those responsible for stock selection. A policy statement may be brief and very general but should guide the building of a suitable collection of books and other material. A sample collection development policy might read as follows:

1. The Library at ABC School supports the curriculum by providing a core of introductory and reference material in all subject areas.

2. The Library will respond to the changing curriculum and to developments in various subject areas through the acquisition of new material.

3. The Library will endeavour to provide a range of books and other material which will represent all view-points on current affairs, problems and issues of the day.

4. Leisure and extra-curricular activities will also be supported by the library through a wide range of fiction and books, magazines and other material on sports and pastimes.

5. Donations of books or other material will be accepted, provided they are in good condition and relevant to the general curricular or extra-curricular requirements of the school, at the discretion of the library staff.

6. The Library will maintain the collection in good order and condition through regular stock editing.

7. The Library will liaise with the local authority public library system and with other school libraries and other information sources in the area, so that students may have access to a wider range of sources.

STOCK SELECTION

Stock selection is the on-going activity of selecting material to meet the needs of students and teachers.

CRITERIA USED FOR STOCK SELECTION

It is useful to make a distinction between fiction and non-fiction, simply because many of the criteria relevant to non-fiction material do not apply to fiction. Non-book materials (audio-visual, multimedia) will be considered separately.

FICTION

Criteria which may be considered when selecting fiction include:
- quality
- possible usage
- language appropriate to students' abilities.

The collection should include works by:
- classic authors
- contemporary authors
- Irish authors
- new authors.

Provision should be made for:
- different age groups
- differing reading abilities
- reluctant readers
- different cultures.

One of the main aims of encouraging fiction reading is to introduce children to a world beyond their own experience. Therefore, the range of fiction should include the following:

- Books in Irish, English and any other language(s) taught in the school or which is the home language of a significant number of students
- Historical novels
- Novels set in different countries and showing diverse cultures
- Fantasy/science fiction
- Fairytales, folk-tales, myths and legends from Ireland and around the world.

Short stories are very useful in encouraging reluctant or less-able readers. They also display the craft of short-story writing.

The emotional, social and physical development of young people should be reflected in the fiction collection. Novels dealing with social issues, e.g. separation, divorce, bereavement, refugees, bullying and drugs should be stocked, as social issues can often be more easily understood when placed in a fictional context.

NON-FICTION

Selection criteria for non-fiction include the following:

- Authority
- Content
- Currency
- Relevance to the curriculum
- Presentation and design
- Potential usage
- Differing abilities
- Language
- Accuracy
- Bibliography
- Index
- Cultural bias
- Price.

Authority

How well qualified is the author to write about the subject? After a number of years, one becomes familiar with known authors in a particular subject and it is not difficult to recognise new talent.

Content

How well does the author cover the subject? What is the value of the material? Does it contribute to the young person's understanding of the subject? Is it intended to be a general introduction to the subject, or an in-depth study of one aspect? Does it stimulate the student to explore the subject further?

Currency

Perhaps the most important criterion when selecting non-fiction material is its currency. Is it up-to-date? Does the text reflect the latest research in a particular subject area?

Relevance to the Curriculum

Books selected should be relevant to the primary school or post-primary school curricula. That is not to suggest, however, that class textbooks should be bought. Rather, the emphasis here is to select books which will provide a wide range of background reading which will widen a student's understanding of a subject or topic. When choosing books in any subject area, attention must be paid to any recent curriculum changes or to changes which may be under consideration.

Presentation and Design

Is it attractive? Is the material organised in a way which makes sense? Is the text broken up into manageable sections, with good use of typeface, bullet-points, text-boxes etc? Is there a good balance of illustration and text? Are the illustrations appropriate to the text, and are they near the relevant passages of text? Are the illustrations varied (if appropriate), e.g. drawings, photographs, diagrams? Do the diagrams have captions? Is the lay-out too 'busy'? Design features should enhance the appeal and readability of a book.

Potential Usage

Books should be bought which will appeal to a wide range of students and teachers. Balancing this, however, one must cater for minority subjects and minority interests across the school.

Care should be taken to stock titles which complement each other, e.g. in a subject area one or two introductory works should be stocked in addition to more detailed works on specific aspects of the subject.

Differing Abilities

The school library must provide material which caters for students with differing abilities. Non-fiction material selected must cater for:

- a range of reading abilities and levels of comprehension
- a range of interest levels.

For students with reading difficulties, there are various non-fiction series available.

Language

When selecting non-fiction material, it is essential to assess books for language complexity. Vocabulary and sentence construction used in some books will be more appropriate to older, more fluent, readers than to those who have reading difficulties. Also, you should ask yourself whether the tone of voice used is likely to stimulate the interest of the reader.

Accuracy

The information contained in the book must be accurate. If in doubt, check with a subject specialist.

Bibliography

The bibliography is a useful means of finding more titles on the subject. A good information book will give suggestions for further reading. Some of the titles mentioned in a bibliography may be available at the local public library.

Index

The index is your key to the information in the book. An index, a glossary and a table of contents are features of a well-produced book.

Cultural Bias

Resources selected for the library should be balanced in terms of reflecting different cultures, religions, races and politics.

Price

Price will influence many selection decisions, not least because few schools in Ireland have a defined budget for library materials. However, value for money in terms of the item itself and also in terms of all the foregoing criteria, rather than simple cost, should be your guiding principle.

REFERENCE MATERIAL

The criteria for reference material are the same as those for non-fiction. However, price, currency and possible usage may be even more important here, as reference books tend to be very expensive. The other criteria – relevance to the curriculum, language, differing abilities, accuracy, content, bibliography and index – should also be considered. On the grounds of cost, currency and flexibility of use, serious consideration should be given to purchasing some reference material on CD-ROM, and allowing access to on-line databases and the Internet.

MAGAZINES/PERIODICALS/JOURNALS

Journals on various subjects will broaden the library's holdings. The criteria for selecting magazines or periodicals are similar to those for non-fiction and reference material. However, potential usage, content, language and authority are very important. Realistically, it would seem that most schools will only take a few magazines and then only for the Transition Year, Fifth Year and Sixth Year classes. Examples of many magazines are available at the local public library so you can assess their relevance for the school.

MULTIMEDIA (ELECTRONIC) MATERIAL

An alternative to buying expensive reference books which may date quickly, is to buy the CD-ROM versions. CD-ROMs are much cheaper, more visually attractive, and often are linked to Internet sites, thus ensuring their currency. It may be easier to obtain funds to buy the hardware so CD-ROMS may be a realistic option for many schools. The selection criteria for CD-ROMs and other software are the same as those for non-fiction and reference material but, in addition, you should consider the following:

- Compatibility with hardware in the library (PC or MAC version?)
- Educational content (particularly important because so many CD-ROMs are so superficially attractive)
- Ease of use – in particular, is it possible to work through the CD-ROM at one's own pace and in one's own way?
- Clear on-screen instructions
- Clear accompanying documentation
- Balance of text, pictures, video-clips, animation
- Sound quality
- Image quality.

AUDIO-VISUAL MATERIAL

The criteria for selecting audio-visual material include the following:

- Needs of school
- Potential usage – either multi-disciplinary or both curricular and extra-curricular
- Image and sound quality
- Content accuracy in the case of non-fiction topics
- Currency
- Supplier reliability
- Possibility of replacement audio-cassette service.

Audio-cassettes or compact discs will be useful for a range of subjects. In addition, cassettes or compact discs (CDs) may be selected for extra-curricular purposes. Possible usage of such material will be high as music and spoken-word cassettes and CDs will be of interest to many students and teachers. It is important to remember that some videos may date. Hair styles and clothes date videos, and can greatly reduce their appeal to students.

SELECTION TOOLS

There are a number of selection tools available. The most widely used are:

- Recommended Reading lists, e.g.

    Children's Book Festival Reading List (annual) – *Best Books* – produced by CBI and the YLG

    The Big Guide to Irish Children's Books (Coghlan, V. and Keenan, C. eds.)

    Book Choice – produced by CBI and the Department of Education and Science
- Annotated reading lists from Local Authority School Library Services around the country
- Reading guides produced by the School Library Association (SLA)
- Review journals or magazines, e.g.
    Children's Books in Ireland
    The School Librarian
    Books for Keeps
    Junior Education
    Child Education
    Times Educational Supplement
    The educational supplements of national newspapers.

All of the above, and many subject specialist journals, will be available for consultation at the local public library or at the School Library Service of the public library system.

ACQUISITIONS

There should be an agreed annual budget for the purchase of resources.

The practical arrangements for buying books will probably be done on an annual, or at most, a term basis. There is no easy formula to decide how much money should be spent on fiction as opposed to non-fiction. The needs will vary from school to school. The following is a recommended place of purchase for various materials:

Daily newspaper:	Local newsagent
Books:	Local bookseller/library supplier
Audio-visual:	Local bookseller/library supplier/specialist AV supplier
Videos:	Specialist AV supplier/library supplier
Music:	Specialist music shop or wholesaler
Magazines/periodicals:	Local newsagent or by subscription.

It is worth checking if other schools in your area have videos. Some schools have set up a system to purchase videos on a co-operative basis. All participants are then entitled to borrow from the common pool of videos. An arrangement such as this will cut down on expenses. However, this must be balanced against the fact that others may need a video at the same time as your school does.

A guiding principle when deciding where to buy material is to start with local suppliers and use suppliers elsewhere if you are looking for something more specialised, or if the local service is not satisfactory.

A good supplier should:

- provide you with a range of current catalogues
- offer a discount
- provide a prompt service
- have a good knowledge of their stock.

Some suppliers provide a processing service for books (laminating paperbacks, for example).

Donations

Donations are often a poisoned chalice. Although offered to the school library for the best reasons, many donated items (usually books) are not suitable for the library, and should be politely but firmly refused.

Book Fairs

Care should also be taken in the area of book fairs, book clubs and special offer promotions. What may seem like a bargain may turn out to be very poor value indeed.

Free Resources

Many useful and attractive resources are available free from a range of sources such as embassies, art galleries, government agencies, commercial companies.

STOCK EDITING

All library material must be weeded periodically. There are practical reasons for this:

- The library has limited space.
- The material has a limited shelf life.
- The stock of the library will not remain relevant forever.

Books should be withdrawn from stock and discarded

- if they are physically worn-out – falling apart, pages missing, etc
- if, in the case of non-fiction, the information is out-of-date.

The following are guidelines as to how often material needs to be weeded:

- Daily newspapers should be discarded after one month. Some newspapers are available in electronic form.
- Local newspapers may be retained for longer periods.

  Before disposing of out-of-date newspapers and journals you may wish to take cuttings.

  Depending on the school's financial resources, you may wish to consider binding local newspapers and journals which will not date too much.

- Yearbooks, annuals and directories should be discarded when you buy the latest edition. However, you may choose to keep local directories for use in Local History projects.

Rebinding

Rebinding may be a possibility for books in poor physical condition.

- The cost of rebinding can be fairly high, so consider alternatives before proceeding.
- Would it be better to buy a newer edition – or another more up-to-date book on the subject?

STOCKTAKING

An accurate record of the number of books and other materials in the school library needs to be maintained so that annual stock audits can then be done easily.

- Stocktaking may be carried out annually in July/August.
- All items issued to staff and students should be recalled before the end of the school's academic year.
- Losses should be noted in the annual report. Gaps can be filled when the new budget is allocated.

COPYRIGHT

Most teachers will be familiar with some books (usually Teacher's Manuals) which are copyright-free, i.e. it is permissible to copy them. These books are usually very clearly labelled.

All other books are covered by copyright.

An author's copyright lasts for the duration of his/her lifetime and for 70 years thereafter. Under the terms of the Copyright Act 1963, the reproduction of these works is restricted. There are some limited exceptions. These include, for example, the making of a single copy of an article for research purposes.

The availability of photocopiers has meant that many people ignore their obligations in relation to copyright. You should familiarise yourself with basic copyright law and alert people to possible copyright infringements. You should discourage students and staff from or unlawful photocopying. Account should be taken of the implications of the Copyright and Related Rights Bill, 1999 and the EU Directive on Copyright.

The Irish Copyright Licensing Agency (ICLA) is responsible for administering the copyright scheme in Ireland.

EVALUATION

Evaluation of a library's collection is an on-going process. Weeding as outlined above is part of the process. The strengths and weaknesses of a collection need to be identified. In terms of a school library, a number of factors will influence evaluation. These include the following:

- Curriculum change
- Students' and teachers' needs
- Students' abilities
- Technological change and the incorporation of new media if appropriate.

Information Skills in the School Library

WHAT ARE INFORMATION SKILLS?

Information skills are the skills of finding and using information effectively. They range from the skills needed to answer a basic enquiry to those needed to conduct in-depth research on a topic. They are fundamental, transferable skills needed by everyone in order to be successful lifelong learners.

Information skills may include the following:

- Using a library
- Asking the right questions
- Listening skills
- Evaluating information
- Communicating information
- Tackling a project
- Study skills.

All of these complement other transferable skills such as literacy, numeracy and IT skills and may be required for all types of enquiry from the simple, closed question (What is the capital of Italy?) to the research project (Tourism in Italy).

LIBRARY SKILLS

The school library should be the main source of information for students, but they will also need to know how to use other libraries, such as the local public library and the libraries of specialist organisations.

Learning to Use the Library

Students need to understand how libraries work. Upper primary and second-level students should be taught the following:

- When the library is open
- How to join a library
    - what are the rules for joining the school library?
    - what are the rules for joining the local public library?
- How to borrow items from the library
- How to reserve items

- What happens if an item is returned late
- What other services are offered by the library, e.g. access to the Internet
- What activities are available in the library, e.g. a homework club, author visits.

The above information should be explained, in simplified form, to infants and junior primary pupils.

The Library Tour

This information could be given in an introductory tour of the library, which, ideally, you should give each class at the beginning of the school year.

The library tour should also explain:

- that books are divided into fiction and non-fiction
- the difference between the two categories
- that fiction is arranged alphabetically by author's surname
- that non-fiction is arranged by subject, usually according to the Dewey Decimal Classification system
- where the library catalogue is situated, and how to use it
- that some items may be borrowed and some are for reference only
- where project and local history files are kept
- where magazines and newspapers are kept
- where audio-cassettes, videos, CDs and CD-ROMs are stored
- where the ICT facilities are situated and what they include
- where new books are displayed.

Areas of the library and resources of particular relevance to a class should be pointed out to that class during their tour. Fiction and leisure reading of interest to the group could also be pointed out.

The Library Guide

The information above could also be presented in a written Guide to Using the Library. This should be given to every student and member of staff. A simple plan or map of your school library (no matter how small or basic the library) is useful for explaining the library layout.

One of the most valuable books on library use is *Library Alive* by Gwen Gawith (see Suggestions for Further Reading at the end of this chapter). This contains a very simple explanation of the Dewey Decimal Classification system as well as exercises and games which could be used with primary school pupils or junior cycle post-primary students to reinforce their library and information skills. Carel Press produces excellent posters and books on the Dewey Decimal Classification system and on information skills in general (see Appendix 4).

SEARCHING FOR INFORMATION

As well as knowing how a library works students need to be able to find and use the information contained in the library. From the simplest enquiry to the most complex piece of research, the same basic techniques apply. Students need to learn:

- how to use the library catalogue
- how to use the subject index
- alphabetical and numerical order.

Students also need to learn different ways of reading a book for information. It should be pointed out to students that they already read different types of text in different ways. For example, many students already know how to **skim** and **browse** but feel that these are inappropriate methods for schoolwork. A good exercise is to ask students to think about how they read the following:

- T.V. guides
- Hobby manuals
- Comics/magazines
- Cookery books.

Demonstrating ways of approaching a book is the most effective way of teaching the skill of extracting information from, and judging the suitability of, a book. If you teach students to look at

- the **title**
- the **subtitle**
- the **contents page**
- the **index**
- the **introduction**
- the **blurb**

and point out all the information to be gleaned from these elements, they will learn how non-fiction books are structured and how to extract from them what is relevant to their needs. In addition, students need to learn how to get information from reference books such as encyclopedias and directories. Above all, the skills needed to extract information from the telephone directory should be taught in a systematic way to students of all ages and all levels of ability. Constant reinforcement of these and other information-seeking methods throughout their school-life will equip students with high-level information skills, skills which will be very valuable to them at all stages of their education.

TACKLING A PROJECT

As well as learning and practising the skills outlined above, students, both in primary and post-primary schools, are required to undertake more extensive enquiries, usually in the form of project work. Any project, no matter how simple, involves research, and that research can and should be taught as a clearly defined process. There are seven stages in any piece of research:

- Planning
- Sourcing
- Selection
- Organisation
- Interpretation
- Presentation
- Evaluation.

These stages are examined in the following pages.

PLANNING

Time Management

Underlying the whole process is the skill of time management. Students should be encouraged to set themselves realistic goals, and to review those goals regularly. Students need to ask themselves, 'How long will this work take?' and 'How long do I have?' The more practice they have doing research work, the more realistic students will become when setting deadlines and scheduling their time.

Choosing a Topic

In those cases where the teacher does not assign the topic, students need to learn techniques for:

- thinking up ideas
- deciding on a topic

and even where the topic has been assigned student need to know how to:

- narrow the focus of the project
- set parameters.

Brainstorming

Brainstorming is one of the best techniques for stimulating ideas. The basic rules of brainstorming are as follows:

- There should not be more than 5 students in a brainstorming group.
- The group should try to think of as many ideas as possible.
- One member (or the teacher) records all contributions.
- No comments or judgements may be made about the ideas.
- Students should forget (at this stage) about practical constraints.

Prior Knowledge

Students should be encouraged to ask themselves, 'What do I already know about this subject?' This is important for many reasons, one being that when students acquire new knowledge they are more likely to understand and remember it if they can relate it to existing knowledge. Another reason is that acknowledgement of their prior knowledge helps the students to see themselves as researchers.

Topic Web

A topic web is a useful way of stimulating and recording ideas about a topic, and of drawing together prior knowledge about the topic. Here is an example:

Thesaurus

Teaching students how to use a thesaurus is another way of helping them to generate alternative and related terms for their research. There are some excellent children's thesauruses available.

The Big Six Questions

Students should ask the 6 questions: Who? What? Why? When? Where? How?

Keywords

Brainstorming, questions and general reflection should produce keywords. These focus the attention of students on the aspect of the topic which they are going to research. Keywords are important for every stage of the research process. A suggested exercise is to have students make **bookmarks** with their keywords on them, to carry with them during their enquiries.

Aims and Objectives

Students need to clarify the aims and objectives of their project.

Aims are broad and often employ the infinitive of the verb, e.g. 'This project aims to find out about the history of fashion in Ireland in the nineteenth century'.

Objectives are more specific and should relate to the overall aim of the project. It is useful to frame them as follows: 'After reading this project, people will know about...' Objectives help students to narrow down their approach so that they don't attempt more than they can manage.

SOURCING

Students need to learn about the variety of sources of information which exists. Now would be a good time to brainstorm again, this time to produce a list of possible sources of information.

The main types of sources are: publications, people, organisations, public libraries and fieldwork.

Publications

As well as learning how to extract information from books, journals, project files and newspapers, students need to learn that the printed word is not the only 'real' source of information. Photographs, television and radio programmes, videos, CD-ROMs and the Internet are all valid sources. Indeed, information from an electronic source is frequently the most up-to-date. However, it should always be stressed that information, from whatever source, must be judged critically and used selectively.

People

Students should be reminded to start with themselves and learn that other people (including family, friends and teachers) are useful sources of information. Newsgroups on the Internet are an interesting source of ideas and opinions.

Organisations

The number and type of organisations that students will come up with depends on the kind of project being done and also on the age and level of ability of the students. In primary school the pupils will usually be considerably more limited in their knowledge of the world outside the classroom. In second-level schools, students should be encouraged to think of the following: libraries; museums; government departments; county council (corporation) services; societies; embassies; companies; protest groups. An essential tool for sourcing organisations is the *Administration Yearbook and Diary* published by the IPA (see Suggestions for Further Reading).

Public Libraries

Students should be aware that the OPAC (Online Public Access Catalogue) in their local public library provides access to the holdings of all the public libraries in the county, and that items can be reserved and obtained through inter-library loan. The local public library often produces a Community Directory listing all the local organisations. It can also be the best place to start when studying local history.

Fieldwork

Included under this heading are the following: observation; sketching and mapping; questionnaires; interviews; surveys. Questionnaires and surveys can be conducted by e-mail. With careful preparation, pupils from first class upwards can undertake fieldwork successfully.

Communication Skills

To get the most from the sources of information students need to develop communication skills. Considerable time and thought should be given to the teaching and reinforcing of these skills.

Telephone Techniques

Role play is probably the most effective way to practice telephone skills. Answering-machines and voicemail are widespread nowadays so students must learn how to leave a coherent message. Students should be reminded to keep a log of their phone calls.

Letter Writing

Students should be taught how to write (by letter or by e-mail) requesting information in a way which is polite and intelligent. Rather than 'Dear Sir, please send me information on vegetarianism for my project which must be in next week,' the letter should specify the relevant aspect of the project and give the recipient time to reply. Wherever possible, letters should be addressed to the Information Officer or Librarian of an organisation.

Students should keep copies of the letters they send and any replies they receive.

Asking Questions

Students should learn how to ask questions in a way which is sensitive and focused, and which takes into account the interviewee's feelings. Questions should not be 'loaded' or confusing. The difference between 'open' and 'closed' questions should be explained. Designing questionnaires is more difficult but involves the same skills.

Listening

Exercises in which students have to practice listening to each other, in pairs and in groups, and then write down or report verbally the key points of what was said, are the best way to develop listening skills.

SELECTION

This is the stage of the process where students must decide what information to use. When faced with the vast range of information available many students panic and photocopy an entire book, or download and print out everything they can from the Internet or CD-ROM. Time and effort at the planning stage pay off now: students should look again at their keywords and use them to assess the **relevance** of the information they have found. They also need to assess the **value** of the information.

Demonstrating ways of evaluating a book, CD-ROM or website, outlining the criteria you use, is a highly effective way of passing on this skill. If you comment aloud on a source of information as you go through it, referring to such concepts as **authority, bias** and **currency**, then students will learn that books and, just as importantly, computers are not infallible and that all information must be critically assessed. This ability to select and reject information can only be developed with practice and encouragement.

ORGANISATION

This is the skill of recording information or making notes. Here again, demonstrating how you would make notes is a useful way of teaching this skill.

Other exercises
- Give students a photocopied text and ask them to highlight the key ideas or facts.
- Ask students to extract specific information from a video (they should be allowed to watch the video at least twice).
- Ask each student to make notes on a set subject and then compare and discuss.

The organisation of information is a matter of personal style, but it is vital that all students practise making notes so that they get the most out of their research.

Bibliography

As they record and organise their information, students should take note of **references**. Even in first class in primary school, pupils should be encouraged to note the title and author of any source they use. As they proceed through school the referencing should become more extensive, for example to include date and place of publication. This then can be linked to the development of evaluation skills.

INTERPRETATION

Referring back to the Planning stage, students should ask the following questions:

- What were my original aims and objectives?
- What were my original questions?
- Have my aims changed now that I've collected information and I've thought a bit?
- Have I got the information I need?
- What have I got?
- What does it all add up to?
- Is anything missing?

A helpful exercise is to use a case study of a 'fictional student'. Present all the bits and pieces of information, ideas, quotes, pictures, diagrams, etc that this 'student' has gathered.

Ask the students to discuss the following:

- Should this student do more research, or at least more thinking?
- How would the class go about synthesising the material?

Using the fictional student method allows the skills of interpretation to be taught without undermining the confidence of real students. There is increasing evidence that younger primary pupils and some second-level students need to have their initial attempts at writing quite heavily 'scaffolded'. In *Writing Frames* by Lewis and Wray (see Suggestions for Further Reading) different examples of such scaffolding are given, and it is suggested that students will, with practice, gain the necessary confidence to devise their own ways of structuring, and making sense of, their findings.

PRESENTATION

There are many ways of presenting research findings. In a school context students are usually required to present their findings in written form, most often in a scrapbook. However, students should brainstorm again in order to think of other possible formats:

- A talk
- A video
- A model
- A tape/slide presentation
- A dramatic presentation
- A song
- A wall display.

Another useful exercise to encourage students to be creative is to ask them to convert projects from one format to another:

- Convert their scrapbook into a tape/slide presentation
- Convert their project into an advertisement
- Convert their song into a debate
- Put their project on the school website.

Audience is an important factor when deciding on format. Ask students to put themselves in the shoes of the person who will be reading or listening to their project. They must **never be boring!** Also, they need to be as **clear** as possible. If they are presenting their findings as written work students should remember the following:

- Have a title page, a contents page, chapters with appropriate headings and a bibliography.
- The chapters should be in a sensible order – the usual sequence is from the general to the particular.
- Don't always use words – use pictures, diagrams, maps.
- Proofread – check and double check one's work.
- The computer is not infallible – using the spellchecker function is not a guarantee of error-free writing.

You should build up a collection of materials in the library to help students with the presentation of their project. It could include the following:

- Books on report writing, layout and design, public speaking, video-editing
- Word processing, spreadsheet and desktop publishing software packages (and clear instructions on how to use them)
- Multimedia authoring packages
- Disks of computer clip art (and clear instructions on how to import them into word-processed work)
- Coloured markers and other materials for artwork
- A laminator or plastic covers.

Examples of good practice should also be made available. For example, you could display previous projects in the library (with the permission of the authors) and arrange visits to events like the Young Scientist exhibition.

EVALUATION

It is very important that students look back at how they did their project so that they can assess their own strengths and weaknesses. This allows for progression. The class could usefully discuss the following:

- The time spent planning
- The resources they used
- Major difficulties encountered
- What they enjoyed doing.

Individually students need to ask themselves:

- What did I learn (skills and knowledge)?
- What did I achieve? How do I rate my work?
- What could I improve in the future?

A WHOLE-SCHOOL PROGRAMME OF INFORMATION SKILLS

Information skills are cross-curricular and are best taught through a whole-school programme which would reinforce skills from year to year. As the person with responsibility for the library you are ideally placed to co-ordinate such a programme, but you should consider the following factors:

- Do you have a clear understanding of what you want in a programme?
- What are the strengths and weaknesses of your school in the area of information skills?
- The support of the school principal and deputy principal is vital.
- The gradual development of a programme, in consultation with all teachers, will be more successful than one presented as a finished product.
- It may be useful to pilot the programme with one class over a school year.
- Any course should be rigorously evaluated and amended where necessary.

RESEARCH SKILLS: A SUMMARY

STAGES OF THE PROCESS	SKILLS THE STUDENT MUST DEVELOP	SKILLS YOU CAN HELP TO DEVELOP
PLANNING	DEFINING THE AIM STATING OBJECTIVES SELECTING KEYWORDS SCHEDULING ONE'S TIME	BRAINSTORMING/GROUPWORK FOCUSING/NARROWING TOPIC TIME MANAGEMENT DRAWING ON PRIOR KNOWLEDGE
SOURCING	LEARNING WHAT SOURCES OF INFORMATION THERE ARE: ■ PUBLICATIONS ■ PEOPLE ■ ORGANISATIONS ■ FIELDWORK OBTAINING INFORMATION	LIBRARY SKILLS COMMUNICATION SKILLS: ■ INTERVIEW ■ LISTENING ■ LETTERWRITING ■ TELEPHONE

SELECTION	SELECTING & REJECTING
	   MATERIAL
	EVALUATING MATERIAL
		EXTRACTING INFORMATION FROM
		   BOOKS
		EVALUATING INFORMATION

ORGANISATION	RECORDING INFORMATION NOTE-MAKING BIBLIOGRAPHY	VARIOUS NOTE-MAKING TECHNIQUES BASIC (AND THEN MORE COMPLEX) BIBLIOGRAPHY
INTERPRETATION	SYNTHESISING INFORMATION COLLECTED HOW TO: COMPARE, CONTRAST, ETC	ANALYTICAL SKILLS
PRESENTATION	SELECTION OF FORMAT AWARENESS OF AUDIENCE USE OF ILLUSTRATION CREATIVITY PROOFREADING	COMMUNICATION SKILLS DESIGN AND LAYOUT WORD PROCESSING & USE OF COMPUTER GRAPHICS

EVALUATION	SELF-EVALUATION	REALISTIC ASSESSMENT OF ONE'S
		   OWN WORK
		REFLECTION ON WHAT HAS
		   BEEN LEARNED
		THINKING ABOUT WHAT COULD
		   BE IMPROVED IN THE FUTURE

SUGGESTIONS FOR FURTHER READING

Dubber, Geoff, *Developing Information Skills through the Secondary School Library,* Swindon: School Library Association, 1999. ISBN 0900641940

Gawith, Gwen, *Library Alive! Promoting Reading and Research in the School Library,* London: A & C Black, 1987. ISBN 0713629002

Herring, James E., *Teaching Information Skills in Schools,* London: Library Association Publishing, 1996. ISBN 185604176X

Institute of Public Administration, *Administration Yearbook and Diary,* Dublin: I.P.A. Annual

Lewis, Maureen and Wray, David, *Writing Across the Curriculum: Frames to Support Learning,* Reading: Reading and Learning Information Centre, University of Reading, 1998. ISBN 070491266X

Lewis, Maureen and Wray, David, *Writing Frames: Scaffolding Children's Non-fiction Writing in a Range of Genres,* Reading: Reading and Learning Information Centre, University of Reading, 1996. ISBN 0704910640

McCafferty, James, *Information Skills 1: Accessing Written Information,* London: Hodder and Stoughton Educational, 1995. ISBN 0340643234

McCafferty, James, *Information Skills 2: Library and Research Skills,* London: Hodder & Stoughton Educational, 1995. ISBN 0340643242

McCafferty, James, *Information Skills 3: Data Handling,* London: Hodder & Stoughton Educational, 1995. ISBN 0340643250

The World Book Pathfinder: A Guide to Information Resources, London: World Book, 1993. ISBN 0716650045

Local Studies

Projects and other activities related to local studies may create demands on school libraries. This will involve decisions about what information should be kept in the library and how it should be housed. Such information will include guide books to the locality, reports from local organisations, biographies of local celebrities and past students, posters, maps, photographs and articles and pictures from local papers and magazines. Video and audio tapes may also form part of a local studies collection.

Books may be kept on shelves but smaller items are best kept in cardboard or plastic wallets or envelopes, box files and hanging files in a filing cabinet. Specific files can be kept for different aspects of a local study, for example:

MAYO – BOGS – FLORA

MAYO – HISTORY – FAMINE TIMES

It will not be necessary to retain all of the information on a long-term basis, so detailed cataloguing may not be required. Instead, a brief entry may be made in the catalogue and items contained in a folder or file may be listed on the outside cover of the file for quick reference, for example:

WATERFORD – REGINALD'S TOWER – HISTORY

This file would contain pamphlets, plans, photographs and articles about the history, conservation and tourist attractions of Reginald's Tower.

The National Library of Ireland produces facsimile packs related to Irish history, for example on the Famine and on Daniel O'Connell. These could also be hung in a filing cabinet.

Records and information relating to the school and its environment may also be kept in the library, but care must be taken that archival material is properly handled and housed, for example in acid-free containers. Many schools have connections with parishes and relevant information about the school building may be found in parish records. These may be found in the local church and more information may be available from the offices of the denomination concerned.

It is also important to know where to send students for further information related to their locality. The public library or local museum or heritage centre will be able to direct them to useful sources. The IPA *Administration Yearbook and Diary* and the following list of useful organisations may be used to locate specific information. Advice given on contacting outside agencies in Chapter 8 'Information Skills in the School Library' should be followed. A number of county historical associations, heritage groups and other agencies relevant to Irish local studies may be found at the *Directory of Irish Sites* http://www.browseireland.com/main.htm.

USEFUL ORGANISATIONS

Bord na Gaeilge, 7 Cearnóg Muirfean, Baile Átha Cliath 2

Catholic Press and Information Office, 169 Booterstown Avenue, Co. Dublin

Central Statistics Office, Ardee Road, Dublin 6

ENFO (The Environmental Information Service), 17 St Andrew Street, Dublin 2

GAA (Gaelic Athletic Association), Páirc an Cróchaigh, Baile Átha Cliath 3

Irish Architectural Archive, 73 Merrion Square, Dublin 2

Irish Peatland Conservancy Council, 119 Capel Street, Dublin 1

Irish Traditional Music Archive, 63 Merrion Square, Dublin 2

Islamic Centre, South Circular Road, Dublin 8

Jewish Community Offices, Dublin 6

Kilmainham Gaol, Kilmainham, Dublin 8

National Archives, Bishop Street, Dublin 2

National Gallery of Ireland, Merrion Square, Dublin 2

National Library of Ireland, Kildare Street, Dublin 2

National Museum of Ireland, Kildare Street, Dublin 2

Ordnance Survey of Ireland, Phoenix Park, Dublin 8

Presbyterian Historical Society, Church House, Fisherwick Place, Belfast BT1 6DW

Public Record Office of Northern Ireland, 66 Balmoral Avenue, Belfast BT9 6NY

Representative Church Body Library, Braemor Park, Dublin 14 (Church of Ireland records)

Wesley House, 1 Fountainville Avenue, Belfast BT9 6AN (Methodist records)

SUGGESTIONS FOR FURTHER READING

Aalen, F. Stout, M. & Whelan, K., (eds.), *Atlas of the Irish Rural Landscape*, Cork: Cork University Press, 1997. ISBN 1859180957

Administration Yearbook and Diary, Dublin: IPA. Annual.

Archaeology Ireland (periodical), Five Acres, The Scalp, Killegar, Enniskerry, Co. Wicklow.

Bogs in the Classroom: a Peatland Resource Pack for Teachers. Irish Peatland Conservancy Council, 119 Capel Street, Dublin 1

Boylan, Henry, *A Dictionary of Irish Biography.* 3rd ed, Dublin: Gill & Macmillan, 1998. ISBN 0717125076

Connolly, J.J., (ed.), *Oxford Companion to Irish History*, Oxford: Oxford University Press. 1998. ISBN 0192116959

Directory of Libraries and Information Services in Ireland, Dublin: Library Association of Ireland. (most recent edition)

Facts about Ireland, Dublin: Department of Foreign Affairs, 1995

Flanagan, D. & Flanagan, L., *Irish Place Names.* Dublin: Gill & Macmillan, 1994. ISBN 071712066X

Gillespie, R. & Hill, M., (eds.), *Doing Irish Local History: Pursuit and Practice,* Institute of Irish Studies, Queen's University Belfast. ISBN 0853896763.

Harbison, Peter, *Guide to the National and Historic Monuments of Ireland* Dublin: Gill & Macmillan, 1992. ISBN 0717119564

History Ireland. (periodical) History Ireland Ltd, P.O. Box 695, Dublin 8

'Irish Heritage' Series, Dublin: Easons

'Irish Treasures' Series, Dublin: Town House

Joyce, P.W., *The Origin and History of Irish Names of Places,* vols. 1–3. Facsimile of 1913 edition, Dublin: E. Burke, 1995. ISBN 0946130116

Lewis, Samuel, *Topographical Dictionary of Ireland,* vols. 1–2 + Atlas. Facsimile of 1837 edition, Galway: Kenny's Bookshop, 1995. ISBN 0906312418

Local Studies 5–13: Suggestions for the Non-specialist Teacher. The Geographical Association, 160 Solly Street, Sheffield S1 4BF

Mitchell, Frank, *Shell Guide to Reading the Irish Landscape,* Dublin: Country House, 1986. ISBN 0946172064.

Simms, A. & Andrews, J.H., *More Irish Country Towns.* Cork: Mercier Press, 1995. ISBN 1856351211

Southcombe, Dianne, *Local History.* Swindon: School Library Association.

Welch, Robert, ed., *Oxford Companion to Irish Literature,* Oxford: Clarendon Press, 1996. ISBN 0198661584

Promoting the School Library

Once the library is up and running in a school, it is important to let it be known that it is there and what services it offers. It will also be appropriate to carry out promotional activities and to hold special events which draw particular attention to the library.

To begin with, the best promotion is a well-organised and efficiently run library which supports and enhances the educational and social aims of the school. This will depend on the implementation of much of what has been outlined in previous sections of this publication.

The following suggests ways of maintaining a good public profile for the library:

Liaison with Staff, Students and Other Interested Groups

- Request regular meetings with senior management.
- Attend staff meetings.
- Form a library committee.
- Keep the management board and the parents' association informed.

Publicity

- Ensure that signs to and within the library are clear and attractive.
- Provide adequate notices listing hours of opening.
- Produce a guide or information sheet outlining the facilities offered.
- Organise posters and publicity material drawing attention to new acquisitions or to special events in the library.

Library Services

- Ensure that whatever services are offered by the library are effective.
- Do not rush to offer services which may be difficult to deliver.
- Ensure that information about services or resources is updated regularly.

Library News

- Put information about the library on the school website.
- Produce a newsletter containing:
  - news of recent acquisitions
  - reviews of books, CD-ROMs, etc;
    ask students, staff, parents, past students to contribute
  - features on displays or resources related to topical subjects
  - comments/suggestions from library users
  - list of members of the library committee.

Using the Library

- Run a library/information skills programme.
- Put information on using the library in the newsletter and on the school computer network.
- Train students to help in the library. Award certificates at the end of a training course.

Displays

Mount displays of recent acquisitions, seasonal or current topics.

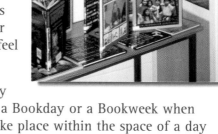

Students, members of staff and parents can all be involved in many of the above activities, e.g. making posters and signs, writing and producing a newsletter, putting information about the library on a website or LAN, mounting displays. This not only lessens the workload on one or two individuals, but also makes others feel a part of the library.

More specific promotional activities may also involve others, and events such as a Bookday or a Bookweek when many of the following activities may take place within the space of a day or a week will require team effort.

PROMOTIONAL ACTIVITIES

Author/Illustrator Visits

- Prepare well beforehand.
- Make sure that students are familiar with the work of the visitor. Plan the visit well in advance.
- Be very clear about the numbers and age group of the students involved.

- Get posters and other relevant publicity material from the publisher of the visitor.
- Make sure the visit doesn't clash with anything else taking place.
- Be on hand to greet the visitor and have some students available also.
- Offer refreshment after the talk/demonstration.
- Arrange financial matters in advance.
- Check if financial support is available from the 'Writers in Schools' scheme organised by Poetry Ireland.
- Check if an author or artist coming from a distance could visit another school or library in the same area to reduce transport costs.
- Ask local bookshops and public libraries to have relevant books available.

Storytellers, Publishers, Other 'Book Related' Visitors

Apply the guidelines for an author visit.

Author Focus

If it is not possible to have a particular author or artist to visit the school, organise an 'Author Focus' instead.

- Gather information about the subject from *Children's Books in Ireland*, *Books for Keeps*, publishers, the local library, biographies, the Internet and from Children's Books Ireland (CBI) if the school is a member.
- Check if the author's books are available on video or audio tape.
- Read and discuss the books.

Visits to a Printer, National Print Museum (Beggars Bush, Dublin), Local Museums or Libraries

Again preparation is essential for a successful visit. Prior to the visit books and relevant artefacts could be displayed and discussed. After the visit the students' reaction to the visit, written and pictorial, might be put on display.

Readings by Teachers, Students, Parents, Local Drama Groups

These will work best if themed. For example, a reading may commemorate an historical event or 'local hero' or be related to a season. Readings might also be related to project work taking place in the school.

Talks/Demonstrations by Local Groups

These might feature specific crafts or skills and may be supported by a display of relevant resources.

Competitions

Quizzes, wordsearch, posters, book covers or book markers.

Desert Island Books

This could be a live event, or it could be recorded on sound or video. Students, teachers, local celebrities could be the subject.

Book Awards (CBI/Bisto, Reading Association of Ireland)

Promote the shortlist by talking about the books listed, or shadowing the Award, i.e. reading the eligible books or the books shortlisted, and picking the winner. The RAI and CBI will give advice on this.

Dramatisation of a Book or Part of a Book

Involve the school drama club or a local theatre group.

Make a Book

Write, illustrate, design, print, bind a book. Learn about the copyright symbol ©, ISBNs (International Standard Book Numbers).

Interviews with Characters from Books

Role-play interview the BFG, Cinderella, Mister Tom, Alice, etc.

Conduct Surveys on What Readers Read

Graphs and tables can be produced to show the results in terms of fiction, non-fiction, poetry, specific categories or genre, etc.

Music in the Library

Invite a local musician(s), feature the students' own music, support with a display of resources.

Create an Advertising Campaign to Promote a Specific Book

Design posters, car stickers, badges, a newspaper radio, television, Internet advertisement.

Parents' Evenings

Invite parents and members of management boards to a talk on the value of reading or to a reading (see above). This could be supported with a display related to some of the above activities.

World Book Day and Children's Book Festival

Some schools choose to celebrate World Book Day (23 April) and the autumn Children's Book Festival with some of these activities. This is a good idea, but there will be extra pressure on authors, illustrators, publishers, libraries and children's books organisations at these times, so make arrangements well in advance. Look out for the World Book Day pack sent free to schools nationwide. It contains a wealth of information about book-related activities.

Useful Contacts

Contact publishers and bookshops for author details, posters, bookmarks and promotional material.

There are also a number of organisations which provide support and resources for promotional activities. These organisations are listed in Appendix 3.

SUGGESTIONS FOR FURTHER READING

Books for Keeps. (periodical), Books for Keeps, 6 Brightfield Road, Lea, London SE12 8QF

Children's Books in Ireland. (periodical), Children's Books Ireland, 19 Parnell Square, Dublin 1

De Saez, Eileen Elliott, *Promoting the School Library.* Swindon: School Library Association, 1997. ISBN 0900641843

Dubber, Elizabeth and Yendall, David, *Display and Publicity for the School Library.* Swindon: School Library Association, 1996. ISBN 0900641789

Gawith, Gwen, *Library Alive! Promoting Reading and Research in the School Library,* London: A&C Black, 1987. ISBN 0713629002

Gawith, Gwen, *Reading Alive!* London: A&C Black, 1990. ISBN 0713632038

McGonagle, Janet, *Promoting Literacy through the Primary School Library,* Swindon: School Library Association, 1998. ISBN 0900641908

Powling, Chris, *Storytelling in Schools ... and Some Stories About it.* Reading: Reading and Language Information Centre, University of Reading. ISBN 0704910683

Local Authority School Library Services

A School Library Service (SLS) to primary schools is provided by the local authorities in conjunction with The Department of Education and Science. Local authorities are responsible for the administrative costs incurred in running SLS, while the Department provides per capita funding, on an annual basis, for the provision of new books for primary school libraries. The grant from the Department of Education and Science for the 1998/1999 school year was £2.15 per pupil, which translated into approximately one new book per year for every 3 pupils (based on an average cost of £10 per book).

The task of librarians in SLS is to select and purchase material suited to the curricular and recreational needs of pupils, including quality fiction, information books, reference books, non-book materials and reading schemes for pupils with reading difficulties.

Schools should ensure that they receive their annual allocations of new books by contacting the SLS in their county at the start of each calendar year. (See Appendix 5 for the names and addresses of county librarians to contact for information about your SLS.)

Nineteen local authorities operate a delivery service to schools. Where no delivery service exists, schools are asked to call into their SLS headquarters to choose and collect their allocations.

Some local authorities supply primary schools with annual allocations of new material which may be kept by schools on a long-term loan basis. This is a way for schools to build up library collections.

Other local authorities provide books on a rotation basis, so that books are lent to individual schools on a short-term basis.

In addition to providing new material, the SLS usually gives professional expertise and advice to primary schools. The level of support given by School Library Services varies from county to county, depending on factors such as staffing and resources.

ADVISORY SERVICES

Advisory services which may be available from your SLS include:

- Planning, setting up and managing new libraries
- Talks to parents, teachers and students on books and reading
- Production of booklists and guides to running a school library

- Information about useful websites and evaluation of educational software
- In-service training in areas such as stock selection, organisation and promotion
- Advice on the selection and use of information technology, i.e. automated library systems, CD-ROM, on-line databases.

REFERENCE FACILITIES

Reference facilities which may be available at your SLS include:

- Display collections of the best books for children
- Published bibliographies and guides to current books for children
- Publishers' catalogues
- Specialist periodicals
- Books on children's literature, reading and school libraries.

PROJECT LOAN COLLECTION

- Non-fiction books for use in project work.
- Items lent on a short-term basis.

DRAMA LOAN COLLECTION

- Playscripts and books about all aspects of drama.

Remember to contact your School Library Service for details about the services on offer.

Appendix 1

LIBRARY ASSOCIATION OF IRELAND – POLICY ON SCHOOL LIBRARIES

1. The Library Association of Ireland in emphasising the crucial role of information provision in education recognises that the school library is:
   - a main source of information in the school
   - the most effective means of ensuring equality of access to the range of learning materials demanded by the curriculum
   - a means of ensuring equality of access to information for students and staff in all schools
   - a means of developing a range of cultural interests, including good leisure reading habits.

2. There should be a statutory obligation to provide effective libraries in schools at all levels. This should be supported by realistic regular financial commitment.

3. The standards outlined in the Library Association of Ireland publication, *School Libraries: Guidelines for Good Practice,* including those relating to facilities, resources, staff and information handling skills, should be regarded as the minimum standards acceptable.

4. All schools should have access to the expertise of a professionally qualified librarian who should liaise with staff and students to exploit and promote the full potential of the school library.

5. Support should be given to the development of the existing local authority school library services to primary schools and to the introduction of similar services to second-level schools. This should include the provision of resources and professional expertise.

6. From the earliest years to school leaving, all pupils should participate in information skills handling programmes which will enable them to become independent, resourceful and successful learners and researchers.

7. Courses in the development and administration of school libraries and information skills teaching should be provided for teachers at pre-service and in-service levels.

Library Association of Ireland, March 1996.

Appendix 2

DUTIES OF THE LIBRARIAN IN THE POST-PRIMARY SCHOOL

To obtain maximum benefit from the library it is essential that the school employs a professionally qualified librarian. It is also important that the librarian is seen as a senior member of the school staff. S/he should have opportunities to liaise with teachers, both formally and informally, and should attend and contribute at staff meetings.

THE LIBRARIAN'S RESPONSIBILITIES WILL INCLUDE:

- evaluating the present level of resource provision throughout the school
- deciding on likely future requirements
- from this, developing a plan for the future of the library and linking this to a library policy
- deciding on and implementing systems for the management and organisation of the library
- financial management and budgetary control for the library
- planning the introduction of computerised cataloguing and circulation systems in the library
- being available to members of staff and pupils who wish to discuss the information requirements of various subject areas and courses
- in conjunction with the teaching staff, developing a programme for a cross-curricular information skills programme at all levels throughout the school
- selecting stock and building a collection
- being aware of new books and other relevant media and developments in ICT
- visiting suppliers and attending exhibitions, seminars and conferences where appropriate
- classifying, cataloguing and indexing stock
- introducing appropriate information technology into the library and having an awareness of how to manage this
- library supervision and counter duties
- promoting the library
- organising library displays and events, e.g. author visits
- dealing with enquiries from staff and pupils
- maintaining project files
- training library assistants
- keeping up-to-date with changes and trends in education
- monitoring the use of the library and applying this to possible future developments.

In addition, a school librarian will need to have excellent communication skills, be self-motivated and have a pro-active attitude to developing and promoting the library.

ANCILLARY STAFF

Some aspects of a school librarians work cannot be carried out when s/he is on duty at the library desk. Therefore, support staff will be required. This may involve employing a part-time library assistant. Such a person will need training in the specific requirements of a school library.

A number of school libraries also train students as 'pupil librarians'. There are some well-established and very successful programmes in action which provide help in the library and also provide pupils with an in-depth knowledge of how libraries work and encourage in them a sense of responsibility.

The duties of support staff include:

- library supervision and counter duties
- processing new stock
- tidying shelves and general tidying in the library
- organising displays
- clerical duties, e.g. typing booklists, sending out overdue notices, making notices
- assisting the librarian in the duties listed above.

Appendix 3

USEFUL ORGANISATIONS

Children's Books Ireland (CBI), 19 Parnell Square, Dublin 1.
Members throughout Ireland. Two copies of *Children's Books in Ireland* each year and notification about recommended reading, children's book events and more. Holds seminars, an annual Conference and Summer School. Reduced admittance for members. Organises the Bisto Book Awards. Annual subscription.

IBBY Ireland PO box 6584, Rathmines, Dublin 6.
Part of the International Board on Books for Young People (IBBY) which encourages understanding through children's books. Works with other national children's book related organisations.

Poetry Ireland, Dublin Castle, Dublin 2.
Facilitates author visits to primary and post-primary schools through the 'Writers in Schools' scheme whereby the cost is shared by the school and Poetry Ireland.

Reading Association of Ireland (RAI), St Attracta's Senior School, Meadowbrook, Ballinteer, Dublin 16.
Aims to stimulate and promote an interest in reading by holding conferences and workshops. Encourages research into reading. Runs the RAI Children's Book Award and the RAI Special Merit Award. Annual subscription.

School Library Association Republic of Ireland (SLARI) is a branch of the School Library Association (SLA), Liden Library, Barrington Close, Liden, Swindon SN3 6HF, UK.
Holds an annual conference and seminars. Invaluable support for anyone involved with a school library. Produces quarterly magazine *The School Librarian*. Publishes *'Guidelines'* series on a range of activities related to the running of a school library. All sold at a reduced price to members. Annual subscription.

Youth Library Group, c/o The Library Association of Ireland, 53 Upper Mount Street, Dublin 2.
Section of the Library Association of Ireland. Holds seminars on a wide range of issues relating to children's books, literacy/reading and youth libraries. Is involved in the organisation of the Children's Book Festival and the production of the CBF reading list. Annual Subscription.

An Chomhairle Leabharlanna (The Library Council),
53 Upper Mount St Dublin 2
Provides advice about practical aspects of running a library: furniture, computerised library systems, etc. Encourages research into all aspects of librarianship.

Appendix 4

DIRECTORY OF SUPPLIERS

Note: This list has been compiled with the help of An Chomhairle Leabharlanna. The editors do not claim that this is a complete list of suppliers or their product ranges. Details are correct as far as is known. Inclusion on this list does not, in any way, constitute a recommendation by the editors, by An Chomhairle Leabharlanna or by the Library Association of Ireland.

AUDIOVISUAL MATERIALS

CONTEMPORARY MUSIC CENTRE,
95 Lower Baggot Street,
Dublin 2.
Tel: 01-6612105
Fax: 01-6762639
Website: http://www.cmc.ie
e-mail: info@cmc.ie

COSMIC SOUNDS,
1A Farenhill Rd.,
Goatstown,
Dublin 14.
Tel: 01-2986551/2986508
Fax: 01-2985715

EVANS, K & M Ltd.,
28 Mary's Abbey,
Dublin 7
Tel: 01-8726855

LINGUAPHONE INSTITUTE (IRELAND) LTD,
41 Upper Abbey St.,
Dublin 1
Tel: 01-8732366
Fax: 01-8732726

MICHAEL A. O'BRIEN (Talking Books),
14 Beechlawn,
Dublin 16
Tel: 01-2987342
Fax: 01-2987342

RONDO,
Unit B10-B12,
Dundonald Enterprise Park,
Carrowcreagh Rd.,
Belfast,
BT1 6OQT
Tel: 0801232-572545
Fax: 0801232-572544

BOOKS

ASKEWS LIBRARY SERVICES LTD.,
25 Pearse St.,
Dublin 2
Tel: 01-6710753
Fax: 01-6774054

BOOKSTOP,
Dun Laoghaire Shopping Centre
Dun Laoghaire
Co. Dublin
Tel: 01-2809917

CAREL PRESS,
4 Hewson St.
Carlisle,
UK
Tel: 0044 1228-538928
Fax: 0044 1228-591816

CARROLL EDUCATIONAL SUPPLIES,
Unit 5,
Western Industrial Estate,
Naas Road,
Dublin 12
Tel: 01-4567279

COLLINS LIBRARY SUPPLY,
Unit 8,
Doughcloyne Industrial Estate,
Wilton,
Cork
Tel: 021-346965
Fax: 021-346955

EBLANA BOOKSHOP LTD.,
4 Slaney Drive,
Dublin Industrial Estate,
Glasnevin,
Dublin 11
Tel: 01-8301111
Fax: 01-8301434

FOLENS SETANTA,
Unit 7,
Broomhill Business Park,
Tallaght,
Dublin 24.
Tel: 01-4515311
Fax: 01-4515306

FRED HANNA LTD.,
27-29 Nassau St.,
Dublin 2.
Tel: 01-6771255
Fax: 01-6714330
Website: http://www.hannas.ie
e-mail: fred@hannas.ie

GREENE'S BOOKSHOP,
16 Clare St.,
Dublin 2
Tel: 01–6762554
Fax: 01–6789091

HODGES FIGGIS,
56/58, Dawson St.,
Dublin 2
Tel: 01-6774754
Fax: 01-6792810

HUGHES & HUGHES
St. Stephens Green Shopping Centre,
Dublin 2.
Tel: 01-4783060
Fax: 01-4750114

INTERNATIONAL EDUCATIONAL SERVICES,
Weston Industrial Est.,
Leixlip,
Co. Kildare.
Tel: 01-6210310
Fax: 01-6210188

IRISH LIBRARY SUPPLIERS LTD.,
270 Lower Rathmines Rd.,
Dublin 6
Tel: 01-4967398
Fax: 01-4960228

MERCIER LIBRARY SUPPLIES LTD.,
18 Academy St.,
Cork
Tel: 021-275040
Fax: 021-270297

O'MAHONY & COMPANY LTD.,
120 O'Connell St.,
Limerick.
Tel: 061-48155
Fax: 061-44558
e-mail: omahonys@iol.ie

Branch outlets:
Lower Shannon
St., Limerick   Tel: 061-49322
Castle St., Tralee   Tel: 066-22266
Abbey St., Ennis   Tel: 065-28355

OPEN BOOK COMPANY
Unit 10,
Kinsealy Business Park,
Kinsealy,
Co. Dublin.
Tel: 01-8463715
Fax: 01-8463661
e-mail: bbannigan@tinet.ie

AN SIOPA LEABHAR
6 Sráid Fhearchair,
Baile Áth Cliath 2
Tel: 01-4783814

SURGISALES/STA LTD.,
252 Harold's Cross Road,
Dublin 6W.
Tel: 01-4966688/4966593
Fax: 01-4966899

WATERSTONES,
7 Dawson St.,
Dublin 2
Tel: 01-6791260
Fax: 01-6791318
e-mail: waterstones@www.uk.com

PERIODICAL SUBSCRIPTION AGENTS

SWETS UNITED KINGDOM LTD.,
32 Blacklands Way,
Abingdon Business Park,
Abingdon,
Oxfordshire OX14 1SX
Tel: 00-44-1235-530809
Fax: 00-44-1235-535055
Website: http://www.swets.nl
e-mail: infouk@swets.co.uk

COMPUTER SYSTEMS/SOFTWARE SUPPLIERS

System: **ALICE**

Supplier: Softlink Europe Ltd.,
26 Hanborough House,
Lodge Road,
Long Hanborough,
Oxfordshire OX7 2LH
Tel: 00-44-1993-883401
Fax: 00-44-1993-883799
Website: http://softlink.com.au
e-mail: alice@softlink.co.uk

System: **AUTOLIB**

Supplier: Payne Automation,
5 Cowper Road,
Berkhamsted
Hertfordshire HP4 3DA
Tel: 0044 1442 873163
Fax: 0044 1442 877440
e-mail: software@pauto.demon.co.uk

System: **CAIRS**

Supplier: Cairs Ltd.,
18-19 Oaklands Park,
Fishponds Road,
Wokingham,
Berkshire
Tel: 0044-1189786880
Fax: 0044-1189786664
Web: http://www.cairs.co.uk
e-mail: cairs@cairs.co.uk

System: **CALM**

Supplier: DS Information Systems Ltd.,
23 Spruce Avenue,
Stillorgan Industrial Park,
Blackrock,
Dublin 18.
Tel: 01-2953035
Fax: 01-2954483
Website: http://www.dsltd.co.uk

System: **CARDBOX**

Supplier: Cardbox Software Ltd.,
Scriventon House
Speldhurst,
Kent TN3 0TU
Tel: 0044-207 4603179
Fax: 0044-1892 863652
Website: http://www.cardbox.co.uk
e-mail: sales@cardbox.net

System: **CLASS**

Supplier: Elizabeth Ford,
11 Colthorp Way,
Thatcham,
Newbury,
Berks RG13 4LW
Tel: 0044-1635 876800

System: **DATA TREK ACADEMIC SERIES**

Supplier: Data Trek UK,
Dugard House,
Peartree Road,
Colchester CO3 5JX
Tel: 0044-1206 369233

System: **ELROND**

Supplier: Head Software Intl,
Croudace House,
97 Godstone Road,
Caterham,
Surrey CRC6RE
Tel: 0044-1883 717057

System: **HERITAGE SCHOOLS**

Supplier: Inheritance Systems,
7 Newtec Place,
66-72 Magdalen Road,
Oxford OX4 1RE
Tel: 0044-1865 200200
Fax: 0044-0865 790853
Website: http://www.inherit.co.uk/
e-mail: sales@inherit.co.uk

System: **INMAGIC** and **CATYLST**

Supplier: Aisling Information Consultants,
77A Marlborough Road,
Donnybrook,
Dublin 4
Tel: 01-4976140
Fax: 01-4976140
e-mail: aislingi@iol.ie

System: **JUNIOR LIBRARIAN** and
MICRO LIBRARIAN

Supplier: Micro Librarian Systems
1st Floor,Priory House,
Ellesmere Avenue,
Stockport
Cheshire SK6 7AN
Tel: 0044-1614 499357
Fax: 0044-1614 499357

System: **LEXICON**

Supplier: Dolphin Computer Services,
5 Mercian Close,
Watermoor,
Cirencester,
Glous GL71LT

System: **LIBRARIAN**

Supplier: Eurotec Consultants,
Aldham House,
Hadleigh,
Ipswich,
Suffolk IP7 6BQ
Tel: 0044-1473 824470
Fax: 0044-1473 824408
Website: http://www.eurotec.co.uk
e-mail: ecl@eurotec.co.uk

System: **LIBRARY PAC**

Supplier: Information Systems Design,
2 Harecourt,
Coventry CV3 3FO
Tel: 0044-1203639129

System: **THE LIBRARY SUITE**

Supplier: DTE Software Systems,
P.O. Box 1322
Bath,
Avon BA1 3TJ
Tel: 0044-1249 445052
Fax: 0044-1249 445053

System: **LICON**

Supplier: Floyd-Ratcliffe,
PO Box 47,
Dorking,
Surrey
Tel: 0044-1306 713181

System: **LIMES**

Supplier: Micoll Computing Ltd,
Rivington House,
82 Great Eastern Street,
London EC2 3JL
Tel: 0044-171 6130037
Fax: 0044-171 7398683
e-mail: limes@compuserv.com

System: **MAC SCHOOL LIBRARY**

Supplier: Celtip Computers,

Apple Centre,
Lower Mill Street,
Kidderminster DY10 2JG
Tel: 0044-1562 822222
Fax: 0044-1562 67202

System: **MICRO LIBRARIAN**

Supplier: Micro Librarian Systems,

Staley House,
Ridge End Fold,
Marple,
Stockport,
Cheshire SK6 7EX
Tel: 0044-1614 499357

System: **MICRO-LIBRARY SYSTEM**

Supplier: Top-Tech Systems
33 Caernarvon Road,
Norwich
Norfolk NR2 3HZ
Tel: 0044-1603 617684

System: **PHOENIX LIBRARY &
RESOURCE MANAGEMENT
SYSTEM**

Supplier: Morgan Barnett Associates,
Lisker House,
Otley,
West Yorks LS21 2DG
Tel: 0044-1943 850537

System: **TELEPEN LIBRARY SYSTEM**

Supplier: SB Electronic Systems Ltd,
Arden Grove,
Harpenden,
HERTS AL5 4SL
Tel: 0044-1582 769991
Fax: 0044-1582 461705
Website: http://www.telepen.demon.co.uk
e-mail: sales@telepen.demon.co.uk

System: **TINLIB**

Supplier: IME,
140-2 St John Street,
London EC1V 4JT

System: **UNICORN**

Supplier: SIRSI Ltd,
Suite A,
Deneway House,
Darkes Lane,
Potters Bar,
HERTS EN6 1AQ,
Tel: 0044-1707 858000
Fax: 0044-1707 858111
Website: http://www.sirsi.co.uk

**AMERITECH LIBRARY
SERVICES LTD.,**
Parkview House,
Beech Hill
Clonskeagh,
Dublin 14
Tel: 01-2602944
Fax: 01-2602698
e-mail:sales@amlibs.ie

**DISKOVERY EDUCATIONAL
SOFTWARE**
18 Lower Liffey St.,
Dublin 1
Tel: 01-8732822
Fax: 01-8732726

GRANT EDUCATIONAL SUPPLIES
73 Bunting Road,
Crumlin,
Dublin 12
Tel: 1800 207020

LIBRARY SHELVING AND OTHER FURNITURE:

Company: **DB OFFICE SUPPLIES,**
Hanover Productivity Centre
Greenstreet East
Dublin 2
Tel/Fax: 01–288 4654

Agency/Product: Terrapin Reska
Gresswell

Company: **DUBLIN BOX COMPANY**
Bluebell Industrial Estate,
Bluebell Avenue,
Dublin 12.
Tel: 01–4500482
Fax: 01–4500634

Company: **EURO-RACK,**
117 Bann Road,
Dublin Industrial Estate,
Dublin 11.
Tel: 01–8307789

Agency/Product: Kasten-Høvik

Company: **DON GRESSWELL LTD.,**
Grange House,
2 Geddings Road,
Hoddesdon,
Herts.
Tel: 00 44 1992–45 45 12
Free fax: 0800 61 66 34
email: direct@gresswell.com
www.gresswell.co.uk

Agency/Products: Bomefa Enem
Softline Xolys

Company: **HOPE EDUCATION**
Kylemore Road,
Dublin 10.
Tel: 01– 6264666
Fax: 01– 626 2628

Agency/Product: Galt Educational
(specialists in equipment for children)

Company: **LFC LIBRARY FURNISHING CONSULTANTS LTD.,**
Ashford House
Tara Street
Dublin 2
Tel: 01–4735220
Fax: 01–4735221

Company: **L.S.& G. DOYLE LTD.,**
Rathdown Road,
Dublin 7.
Tel: 01–868 0875

Agency/Product: Remploy Profile

Company: **MAXI STOR SYSTEMS LTD.,**
Hills Industrial Estate,
Lucan
Co. Dublin.
Tel: 01–628 0291
01–628 0292
Fax: 01–628 0293

Agency/Product: Terrapin Reska

Company: **NEW AGE SERVICES LTD.,**
The Island Business Park,
Chapelizod,
Dublin 20.
Tel: 01–623 2277
01–623 2610
Fax: 01–623 2992
Product: Terrapin Reska

Company: **NIMBLE FINGERS**
Stillorgan
Co. Dublin
Tel: 01–2880788
Fax: 01–2832630

Company: **PETAL POSTFORMING LTD.,**
Dun Fanoir,
Stillorgan Road,
Blackrock,
Co. Dublin.
Tel: 01-2832333
Fax: 01-2832439

Agency/Product: Interdane

Company: **RYCO LTD.,**
Unit 10,
The Craft Centre,
Cornelscourt,
Dublin 18.
Tel: 01-2897912
Fax: 01-2897913
Agency/Product: Book Covers

Company: **SHAPED SYSTEMS LTD.,**
Dearpark,
Boyle,
Co. Roscommon.
Tel/fax: 079-62440

Company: **S.O.S. GROUP,**
Westway Business Park,
1, Apollo Road,
Boucher Road,
Belfast BT12 6HP.
Tel: 08 01232-661133
Fax: 08 01232-682616

Agency/Product: Balmforth Remploy /
Profile

Company: **SPERRIN METAL PRODUCTS
(IRELAND) LTD.,**
49 Seven Oaks,
Dublin 9.
Tel: 01-837 3741
Fax: 01-836 9471

Company: **STORAGE SYSTEMS LTD.,**
Coolock Industrial Estate,
Dublin 17.
Tel: 01-8470956
Fax: 01-847 9892

Agency/Product: BC Inventar

Company: **THOMOND SUPPLY,**
PO Box 58,
19 Henry Street,
Limerick.
Tel: 061-400266
Fax: 061-400313
e-mail: thomond@iol.ie

Appendix 5

LOCAL AUTHORITY SCHOOL LIBRARY SERVICES
LIST OF NAMES AND ADDRESSES

Carlow County

Carlow County Library,
Dublin St,
Carlow.
Tel: 0503–40080; 31126 Ext.217
Fax: 0503–41503

Cavan County

Cavan County Library,
Farnham St,
Cavan.
Tel: 049–31799
Fax: 049–31384

Clare County

Clare County Library,
Library H.Q.,
Mill Road,
Ennis,
Co.Clare.
Tel: 065–21616
Fax: 065–42462
e-mail: Clarelib @ iol.ie

Cork City

Cork City Library,
Executive Librarian,
Grand Parade,
Cork.
Tel: 021–277110
Fax: 021–275684
e-mail: cork.city library @indigo.ie

Cork County

Executive Librarian,
Cork County Library,
Farranlea Road,
Cork.
Tel: 021–546499
Fax: 021–343254

Donegal County

Branch Librarian,
Donegal County Library,
Rosemount,
Letterkenny,
Co.Donegal.
Tel: 073–35380
Fax: 074–26402
e-mail: dglcolib@iol.ie

Dublin Corporation

Children's and Schools' Library Service,
C/O Kevin Street Public Library,
Lr. Kevin Street,
Dublin 8.
Tel: 01–4758791
e-mail: schollib@iol.ie

Dun Laoghaire/Rathdown

County Council,
Duncairn House,
14 Carysfort Ave.,
Blackrock,
Co. Dublin.
Tel: 01–2781788
Fax: 01–2781792
e-mail: strappe@dlrcoco.ie

Fingal County Council

School Library Service,
Unit 34 Coolmine Industrial Estate,
Coolmine,
Dublin 15.
Tel: 01–8225056
Fax: 01–8221568
e-mail: finsclib@indigo.ie

Galway County

Assistant Librarian,
Galway County Library,
Island House,
Cathedral Square,
Galway.
Tel: 091–562471
Fax: 091–565093

Kerry County

Kerry County Library,
Tralee,
Co. Kerry.
Tel: 066–21200
Fax: 066–29202

Kildare County

Kildare County Library,
Athgarvan Road,
Newbridge,
Co. Kildare.
Tel: 045–431109/431486
Fax: 045–432490
e-mail: bgleesen@tinet.ie

Kilkenny County

Kilkenny County Library,
6 John's Quay,
Kilkenny.
Tel: 056–22021 or 22606
Fax: 056–70233
e-mail: kaylib3@iol.ie

Laois County

Laois County Library,
County Hall,
Portlaoise.
Tel: 0502–22044

Leitrim County

Leitrim County Library,
Ballinamore,
Co. Leitrim.
Tel: 078–44012
Fax: 078–44425

Limerick County

Limerick City Library,
Schools Section,
The Granary,
Michael Street,
Limerick.
Tel: 061–314668–415799
Fax: 061–415266

Longford County

Longford County Library,
Longford Town.
Tel: 043–41124
Fax: 043–41125
e-mail: longlib@iol.ie

Louth County

Louth County Library,
Roden Place,
Dundalk.
Tel: 042–35457
Fax: 042–37635

Mayo County

Mayo County Library,
Mountain View,
Castlebar, Co. Mayo.
Tel: 094–24444 Ext 532
Fax: 094–24774

Meath County

Meath County Library,
Railway Street,
Navan, Co. Meath.
Tel: 046–21134

Monaghan County

Monaghan County Library,
The Diamond,
Clones,
Co. Monaghan.
Tel: 047–51143
Fax: 047–51863

Offaly County

Offaly County Library,
County Library H.Q.
O'Connor Square,
Tullamore.
Tel: 0506-46834
Fax: 0506-52769
e-mail: secretar@offalycoco.ie

Roscommon County

Schools' Librarian,
Roscommon County Library,
Abbey Street,
Roscommon.
Tel: 0903-37273
Fax: 0903-25474
e-mail: roslib@iol.ie

Sligo County

County Librarian,
Sligo County Library HQ.
Westward Town Centre,
Bridge Street, Sligo.
Tel: 071-47190
Fax: 071-46798

South Dublin County Council

Unit 1,
The Square Industrial Complex,
Tallaght,
Dublin 24.
Tel: 01-4597834
Fax: 01-4597872

Tipperary County

Tipperary County Library,
Castle Avenue,
Thurles,
Co. Tipperary.
Tel: 0504-21555
Fax: 0504-23442
e-mail: tipplibs@iol.ie

Waterford City

Waterford City Library,
Lady Lane,
Waterford City.
Tel: 051-873501
Fax: 051-50031

Waterford County

Waterford County Library,
Lismore,
Co. Waterford.
Tel: 058-54128
Fax: 058-54877

Wicklow County

County Librarian,
Wicklow County Library,
U.D.C. Offices,
Boghall Road,
Bray, Co.Wicklow.
Tel: 01-2866566
Fax: 01-2865811

Westmeath County

Westmeath County Library,
Dublin Road,
Mullingar,
Co. Westmeath.
Tel: 044-40781/2/3
Fax: 044-41322

Wexford County

Wexford County Council,
Library Management Services,
The Kent Building,
Ardcavan,
Co. Wexford.
Tel: 053-24922
Fax: 053-21097

Appendix 6

FRIENDS OF SCHOOL LIBRARIES

AMERITECH LIBRARY SERVICES LTD

ASKEWS LIBRARY SERVICES LTD

ASSOCIATION OF SECONDARY TEACHERS IRELAND

BORD GÁIS

BUS ÉIREANN

CHIVERS

COLLINS LIBRARY SUPPLY

COSMIC SOUNDS

D.B. OFFICE SUPPLIES

DISKOVERY EDUCATIONAL SOFTWARE

DS INFORMATION SYSTEMS LTD

DUBLIN BOX COMPANY LTD

EBLANA BOOKSHOP LIMITED

FOLENS SETANTA

HODGES FIGGIS

HUGHES & HUGHES

INDEPENDENT NEWSPAPERS

INTERNATIONAL EDUCATIONAL SERVICES

IRISH LIBRARY SUPPLIERS

IRISH NATIONAL TEACHERS' ORGANISATION

KINGSCOURT PUBLISHING LTD

LFC – LIBRARY SUPPLIES AND FURNISHING

LINGUAPHONE INSTITUTE (IRELAND) LTD

MERCIER LIBRARY SUPPLIERS

O'BRIEN PRESS LTD

MICHAEL A. O'BRIEN

O'MAHONY AND COMPANY LTD

OPEN BOOK COMPANY

PENGUIN CHILDREN'S BOOKS

RADIO TELEFÍS ÉIREANN

RONDO

TARA LIBRARY SUPPLIERS

SOFTLINK EUROPE LTD

SWETS UNITED KINGDOM LTD

WATERSTONES

Appendix 7

A NOTE ON THE CONTRIBUTORS

All the contributors are members of the School Library Development Committee, a sub-committee of the Library Association of Ireland.

Carleton Reynolds, Mary, DLIS, ALAI, is County Librarian, Longford County Council. She was co-ordinator of the Caper (Children and Parents Enjoy Reading) Research Project run in conjunction with the Department of Education in Primary Schools in County Longford. She is a founding member of the Youth Library Group (YLG) and jointly edited *School Libraries: Guidelines for Good Practice* (LAI 1994).

Coghlan, Valerie, MSc(Econ), FLAI, FLA, is Librarian at the Church of Ireland College of Education. She is a current Vice-President of the Library Association of Ireland, a member of the Executive of the School Library Association and of the committee of the Republic of Ireland Branch of the School Library Association. She is a founder member and former President of the Children's Literature Association of Ireland, and a founder member of Children's Books Ireland (CBI) and of IBBY Ireland. She has jointly edited *School Libraries: Guidelines for Good Practice* and *The Big Guide to Irish Children's Books* (ICBT 1996). She has written and lectured on children's books and on school libraries in Ireland and abroad and is involved with in-service education related to school libraries.

Kilcline, Helen, BA, FLAI, ALAI, is County Librarian in Roscommon. She formerly worked with Limerick County Library and with Galway County Library as Schools' Librarian. She is the author of *Galway Authors* (1976) and of *Roscommon Authors* (1978) and has contributed articles to various professional publications.

Lonergan, Pat, BA, FLAI, ALAI, is Assistant County Librarian with Kildare County Library. He previously worked with Dublin City Libraries and Dublin County Library. He is a member of the Executive Board of the Library Association of Ireland and is the current Honorary Secretary of the Assistant Librarians' Section of the LAI.

O'Riordan, Gobnait, MA, DLIS, is Project Manager for the Library and Information Services building at the University of Limerick. She previously held the post of WebEditor, University of Limerick and was Librarian, Faculty of Education at the University. She is consultant to the National Sports Information Service at the National Coaching and Training Centre. She is a member of the Executive Board of the Library Association of Ireland. She is the Irish representative on EUROLOG, the European On-Line Users' Group and IASI, the International Association for Sports Information.

Quigley, Patricia, BA, DLIS, HDipAdEd., ALAI, is Librarian at the City of Dublin VEC Curriculum Development Unit (CDU). In addition she is co-ordinating editor for all CDU publications. She has been involved with in-service training for post-primary teachers and adult education tutors for many years, mainly in the areas of information skills and self-directed learning. She has also written on these topics for various publications, including *Library Development in Second-Level Schools* (LAI 1994).

Sliney, Marjory, MSocSc, DipLib(Wales), ALA, ALAI, is Senior Librarian with Fingal County Libraries and is currently responsible for Acquisitions and Development. In the early 1980s she set up and developed the Library at Ballinteer Community School as pilot scheme for Dublin County Library Service. Since then she has been involved with in-service training for both primary and post-primary teachers. She is a reviewer for the Library Association Record. Currently a Vice-President of the Library Association of Ireland, she has represented the Association at international meetings and is its representative on the committee of NEWSPLAN.

Turley, Liz, BA, HDipEd, DLIS, is Senior Librarian in Dublin City Public Libraries. She is currently in charge of the Children's and Schools' Section. She was Chairperson of the Library Association Ad Hoc Committee which drew up the National Policy Statement on Library Services for Children and Young People. She is a committee member of IBBY Ireland.

Walton, Rosemary, MA, HDipEd, DipLib, ALA, ALAI, is Senior Librarian with Dublin Corporation Public Libraries and was formerly in charge of the Children's and Schools' Section. She is the current Chairperson of the Youth Library Group, Library Association of Ireland and was involved in drawing up the LAI Policy on Library Services for Children and Young People. She has served on the judging panel for the CBI/Bisto Book of the Year Award. She has contributed a chapter to *The Big Guide to Irish Children's Books* and co-edited *School Libraries: Guidelines for Good Practice.*